This is the Mass

This is
THE
MASS

NEW AND REVISED

as described by Henri Daniel-Rops

as celebrated by Fulton J. Sheen

as photographed by Yousuf Karsh

Translated, with annotations, by Alastair Guinan

With an introduction and a foreword to the
New and Revised Edition by Bishop Sheen

HAWTHORN BOOKS, INC.
Publishers · New York

H-9338

DI SUA SANTITA

SECRETARIATE OF STATE OF HIS HOLINESS,
THE VATICAN, 3 MAY 1952 (n.275829).

SIR:

The Holy Father has duly received the handsomely bound copy of your little work on the Mystery of the Altar, *Missa Est*, which you sent to him in a spirit of filial respect.

I am happy to tell you that he is well pleased with this book in which you continue your praiseworthy efforts to communicate, and widely to diffuse, the Christian spirit by explaining to your readers the meaning and significance of the various parts of the Mass. His Holiness trusts that your book will convey to its readers those insights which will help them to a fuller sharing in the Holy Sacrifice; and that end, doubtless, will be the best recompense the book's author could desire. The Sovereign Pontiff gladly renews, at this time, his Apostolic Blessing to you, as an expression of his paternal encouragement of your work, and of his gratitude for your filial greetings.

Be assured, Sir, of my own sincere good wishes.

J. B. MONTINI

Sosituto

MONSIEUR DANIEL-ROPS,
NEUILLY-SUR-SEINE.

5

Foreword

WE CHANGE OUR CLOTHES, but our personalities remain. Liturgy changes, but the Mass is the same. Since the first edition of this book, the Bishops of the United States have introduced changes in the Mass on November 23, 1964, and again on March 7, 1965. Principal among these changes was the use of English. This is actually not as much of an innovation as it would seem. Latin was once the language of many parts of Europe. In other words, the Mass was in the vernacular. Putting part of it into English, now, is merely a return to talking to God in one's own tongue.

Other changes were added, but most of them were directed to an increased participation on the part of the laity. A Communion rail to some seemed like a "footlight" dividing the priest and the people, as the actor and the audience. But the liturgy itself never shared this divorce of the Sacrifice and the people because the Mass is the sacrifice of the Mystical Body of Christ, or the "People of God." For that reason the Church was always insistent that a server be present, for he was not there to be just helpful in handing wine and water, but to be a representative of the congregation.

Furthermore, the new liturgy, with the closer union of priest and people, will make the Mass more and more a re-enactment of Calvary, where Johns and Marys will be spoken to from the Cross, as they were on Golgotha; where words of mercy will be extended to thieves who creep into the pews; where all humanity in the Name of Christ will intercede to the Father for the remission of sins; and where the thirst of the people will be quenched by the wine that germinates virgins.

MOST REVEREND FULTON J. SHEEN, D.D., Ph.D.
National Director of the Pontifical Society
for the Propagation of the Faith

Translator's Foreword

THE VERY FAVORABLE RECEPTION given by English-speaking readers to the first edition, published in 1958, of this translation of M. Henri Daniel-Rops' noble commentary on the Mass, enhanced as it is by Mr. Yousuf Karsh's superb photographs of an eminent American prelate, the Most Reverend Fulton J. Sheen, in the act of celebrating the Eucharist, has encouraged the publishers to hope that a new edition might meet with an equally generous welcome not only from those who have, during the past seven years, found the book useful, but also from other thoughtful readers in whom the actions of the late Pope John, of the Vatican Council, and of His Holiness Pope Paul VI, in appealing to all men of good will, may have aroused a desire to understand what is really at the root of Catholicism in the modern world, and a willingness to comprehend the contribution, fed from the very heart of the matter, which the Church stands ready to make to a world which it has not ever forsaken but which it hopes, increasingly, to redeem.

The entire text and the notes have been carefully reviewed and, wherever necessary, rewritten in order to bring the book into accord with the latest developments in the liturgical enactments of authority and with the findings of a scholarship ever widening and continually opening new approaches to one of the oldest acts of individual and social religious concern known the world over. A new arrangement of certain chapters has been devised to meet rubrical changes authorized this year; a new chapter has been inserted to explain the Homily or Sermon, which the Council, revivifying traditional practice, wishes to see closely knit to the total act of worship of which it is a part; and new photographs have been provided wherever that was deemed helpful to the clarification of changes in ceremonial structure written into the new *Ordo Missae* published at the Vatican in 1965. The author of the book, M. Daniel-Rops, of the French Academy, was most kind in his generous response to suggestions that he make changes in his original text where recent developments require that this be done; and I would say an especial word of thanks to His Excellency, Bishop Sheen, and to Mr. Karsh, who, in the midst of their taxing schedules, have made time to co-operate with us.

My own contribution to the volume has been made easier by assistance and advice given me by several friends who have allowed me to impinge upon their time and knowledge. I wish particularly to thank the Very Reverend Austin Vaughan, S.T.D., of the Faculty of St. Joseph's Seminary at Dunwoodie, New York, who showed as much painstaking interest in the revision as many busy men would give to a work of their own. The Reverend William G. LaVerdière, S.S.S., of the Church of St. Jean Baptiste, New York; the Right Reverend Timothy Flynn, P.A., Secretary for Communications for the Archdiocese of New York; the Very Reverend Florence D. Cohalan, M.A., of Cathedral College, New York; the Reverend Edward R. Daley, O.P., Secretary to the Prior Provincial of the Order of Preachers in New York, have graciously answered questions on special points about which I needed information. Miss Alice Kidney McLarney, M.A., of the Department of English at Hunter College, herself a poet, was good enough to give me some counsel in respect to my attempts to cast the original French free verse passages, scattered here and there throughout the book, into what are, it is hoped, acceptable English renditions of the sentiments which they embody. I have also to thank Thomas Boyd Kenedy, Esq., of the firm of P. J. Kenedy & Sons, New York; Maurice Lavanoux, Esq., Secretary of the Liturgical Arts Society, New York; and the Trustees of the Library of St. Bede, New York, for their kindness and generosity in allowing me the use of certain books for reference and consultation.

And it is with real pleasure that I express my indebtedness, for many kinds of help and most useful suggestions, to Dr. Rose-Marie Daële, *Officier dans l'Ordre des Palmes Académiques,* Chairman of the Department of Foreign Languages at Hunter College High School of the City University of New York, and Professor at the French University in New York. In 1957, when my original translation was first undertaken, my Mother was still living, and she provided me with help not only in the construction of the English version itself but in numerous details; and my wife, Dr. Daële, has now assisted me in like manner in preparing this new version of *This is the Mass.*

For any errors which may have escaped the vigilant eyes of my collaborators, I am alone responsible, as also for such opinions as I have expressed upon points which may be matters of contention and controversy among students of liturgiology.

ALASTAIR GUINAN

New York, Feast of the Assumption
of Our Lady, 1965

Contents

The Sacrifice
of the Mass

SOME THINGS IN LIFE are too beautiful to be forgotten. These things may be what men do in this world; they may even be their manner of passing from it. For example, almost every country has instituted a memorial day to recall the supreme sacrifice its patriots have made in defense of country and civilization. Because life was the most precious thing they could give, the living cannot forget their gift. They themselves could not ask for any such memorial, nor could they institute it; that was left to their survivors.

If it is fitting that we have memorial days for those who died to preserve freedom from the oppression of men, it is fitting, too, that there be a memorial for the supreme sacrifice of Christ Who died to give us freedom from the tyranny of sin. There are many differences, however, between those patriots and Christ. No one of them was born to die; each was born to live and death was for each a brutal interruption. But Our Lord came to die; it was the goal of His life, it was the goal He was seeking. For no other purpose came He into the world than to redeem sinful humanity.

Furthermore, unlike the men who could not make their own memorial, He instituted the precise way in which His death was to be recalled. Since He came to die, this death was the chief thing He wished us to remember. He did not say that men should write a history of it, or even that they should be kind to the poor in memory of Him; He gave them the exact manner in which He wished this sacrifice to be commemorated. The memorial He gave us is called the Mass.

It was instituted the night before He died at what has since then been called the Last Supper. Taking bread into His hands He said: "This is my body, which is to be given for you," that is, the next day on the cross. Then over the chalice of wine, He said: "This is my blood, of the new testament, which is to be shed for many to the remission of sins." He was a priest offering Himself as a victim so that men might never forget that "greater love than this no man hath than that he lay down his life for his friends." And after prefiguring and foreshadowing the way in which He would die the next day for the redemption of the world, He gave the Divine command to His Apostles and to His Church: "Do this for a commemoration of Me." In that Last Supper He looked *forward* to the Cross; in the Mass we *look back* to it.

The Mass is the application and the projection through space and time of the redemptive love of Christ on the Cross. Imagine a radio station sending out messages from all eternity, it is there all the time but we only hear the messages as we begin to tune in. So, too, the sacrifice that was offered on the Cross has an eternal value, but the Mass helps more and more people to "tune in" on its merits and to apply them to themselves.

The Redemption of Our Lord on the Cross was offered once for all, but its actualization has depended upon the unfolding of history. Potentially every human being in the world was redeemed on the cross; the actualization and the application of that redemption depends upon the free cooperation of man in the course of history.

Calvary took up only a moment of time, but being the sacrifice of the Eternal God made man, it was capable of illumining the whole of time in all periods of history. The Mass is the projection in time of the eternal values of Calvary.

Similarly Calvary was only one small place on the earth at the crossroads of Jerusalem, Athens and Rome, but what took place there, the sacrifice of the Omnipotent, can affect man everywhere in all corners of the earth. The Mass plants the cross in a town, in a village, in a mission, in a great cathedral; it draws back the curtains on time and space and makes what happened on Calvary happen there. The cross affected all past history by *anticipation;* all the sacrifices of bullocks, and goats, and sheep, and particularly the sacrifice of the paschal lamb, found their completion in the cross. The cross affected also the *future,* by flowing out through all time, like a mighty waterfall or cascade which makes channels through valleys and plains.

The very fact that all sacrifices practically ceased after the sacrifice of Calvary, meant that Calvary was the perfection and the fulfillment of *all* sacrifices. Even the Jews no longer sacrifice paschal lambs in their synagogues, for the True Paschal Lamb has already been sacrificed.

The sacrifice of the Cross, therefore, is not something that happened more than 1900 years ago, it is something that is still happening. It is not an heirloom or an antique which endures into the present; it is a drama as actual now as then, and so it will remain as long as time and eternity endure.

On the Cross Our Blessed Lord knew how every individual soul in the world would react to His supreme act of love, whether or not they would accept Him or reject Him. We ourselves do not know how we will react until we are confronted with Christ and His Cross, and we see it unrolled on the screen of time. From our point of view, it takes time to see the drama unfolded. But the Mass gives us an intimation; we were not conscious of being present on Calvary on Good Friday, but we are consciously present at the Mass. We can know something of the role we played at Calvary by the way we act at the Mass in the twentieth century, and by the way the Mass helps us to live.

The Mass is not a *new sacrifice* but another *enactment* of the one supreme sacrifice of Calvary. There are two moments in history, one when the sacrifice is expected and the other when the sacrifice is possessed and offered. The first moment is called B.C., the second moment is called A.D.

If the Blessed Mother and St. John at the foot of the Cross had closed their eyes when Our Lord was offering Himself for the sins of the world, the spiritual effects on them would have been no different from those which we may receive as we assist at the Sacrifice of the Mass. But if their eyes were open, there would have been this difference: they would have seen the sacrifice offered in bloodshed with blood pouring from gaping holes in hands and feet and side. In the Mass, we see it performed without bloodshed.

The Mass, therefore, is not a substitute for the Cross, but the merit we gain at the Mass is the same as the merit we would have gained if we had assisted at Calvary.

The reason there is only one sacrifice, is that the Priest and the Victim both on the Cross and in the Mass, are one and the same person. Up until the coming of the Son of God, there were many sacrifices offered for sins. Men felt that they were unfit to exist before the Divine Presence. By taking the life of an animal or by destroying a thing, they vicariously punished and purified themselves. Among all peoples, in addition to the Jews who had the great advantage of Divine revelation, there were therefore, priests who offered victims of sacrifice. Their task was to slay the goat or the sheep, or pour out the wine, or immolate the bull. But when Our Lord came He became at one and the same time *Priest* and *Victim*, He became both the Offerer and the One Who was offered. No longer were the priest and victims *separate* as they had been before. On the Cross, therefore, He was upright as a Priest; He was prostrate as a Victim because He was offering Himself.

The Priest offers the Mass only as the representative of Christ, hence he does not say, at the moment of consecration, this is the Body and Blood of Christ but "This is My Body" and "This is My Blood"; he is only an instrument of Christ in the same way that a pencil is an instrument of one who writes.

We said that one of the differences between the Cross and the Mass was that in the Mass the sacrifice is offered without bloodshed, whereas on the Cross there were the heart-rending scenes of Crucifixion. A second difference is that on the Cross Our Lord was alone while in the Mass we are with Him. How we are with Him, will be made clear if we examine the Offertory, the Consecration and the Communion.

OFFERTORY

In order to apply the merits of redemption to our souls we must recapitulate in ourselves the death to sin which was brought about on the Cross. Hence, the first act is the offering of ourselves in union with Christ. In the early Church this was done by offering the very same elements which Our Lord Himself offered at the Last Supper; namely, bread and wine. In the early Church the faithful brought bread and wine to the Mass and some of each was used by the priest for the sacrifice. There are some intrinsic reasons why these elements should have been used, even apart from their Divine authorization. First, bread and wine had been the traditional nourishment of most men through history. Bread, as it were, is the very marrow of the earth and wine is as its very blood. The faithful, therefore, in offering that which has given them their physical sustenance and life, are equivalently giving themselves. A second reason is that no two substances in nature better represent unity than do bread and wine. Bread is made from a multiplicity of grains of wheat, wine from a multiplicity of grapes. So the faithful, who are many, combine to make one offering with Christ. A third reason is that few elements in nature better symbolize sacrifice than wheat and grapes. Wheat does not become bread until it has passed through the Calvary of a winter and has been subjected to the tortures of the mill. Grapes do not become wine until they have trodden the Gethsemane of the wine press. Today, the faithful no longer bring bread and wine to the Sacrifice of the Mass but they bring the equivalent; that is the reason why the collection is often taken up at what is called the Offertory of the Mass. The material sacrifice which they make for the Mass is still a symbol of their spiritual incorporation in the death of Christ. Though they bring no bread and wine, they bring that which buys bread and wine, and these elements still represent the material of their united sacrifice.

CONSECRATION

We have offered ourselves to God as Our Lord offered Himself to His Heavenly Father. The essence of Christianity is the reproduction of what happened to Our Blessed Lord in the life of every single person in the world. The human nature which He took was the pattern, or model nature, for all of us. As He was crucified, rose again and ascended into glory for the redemption of the world, so every person is to offer his human nature freely to Our Blessed Lord and to die to sin in order to live in grace and glory with Him. The Mass represents the peak of that incorporation into the death and glory of Christ. In the Offertory we present ourselves to God under the form of bread and wine.

Now we come to the Consecration, when what is known as Transubstantiation takes place. We are beginning to die to the lower part of ourselves in order to live to Christ. Transubstantiation means that when the words of Consecration are pronounced, the substance of the bread becomes the substance of the Body of Christ, and the substance of the wine becomes the substance of His Blood. It has for its effect a new presence without bloodshed, of the offering of Calvary. In the Mass, there is not another offering, but only another presence of the same offering through the ministry of the priest.

The bread and wine are not consecrated together but separately. First the bread which becomes His Body, then the wine which becomes His Blood. This separate consecration of the bread and wine is a kind of mystical separation of His Body and His Blood, equivalent to the way He died on Calvary.

The consecration of the Mass does not mean that Our Lord dies again, for He never can die again in His own individual human nature, which is now in glory at the right hand of the Father. But He prolongs His death in us. That is one of the reasons that there must always be a servant or server, a member of the Church in attendance when the Mass is said. The Mass is the offering of the living Church and its faithful. It is almost as if at the moment of consecration Our Lord were saying: "I cannot die again in My human nature which is in glory at the right hand of the Father, but Peter, Paul, Mary, James, Ann: you give Me your human nature and I will die again in you." In the Offertory we presented ourselves for sacrifice with Christ; in the Consecration we die with Him. We apply His death to ourselves that we may share His glory. The eternal now breaks in upon the temporal and there is nothing more solemn on the face of the earth than the awe-inspiring moment of consecration. It is not a prayer, it is not a hymn, it is not something said, it is a Divine act which enables us to apply the Cross to ourselves.

Though primarily the words of consecration mean that the Body and Blood of Christ is present on the altar, there is a secondary meaning which concerns ourselves. The priests and the people are also called to make such a total dedication of themselves, by death to sin and lower life, that they can say: "This is my body, this is my blood. I care not if the species or the accidents or the appearances of my life remain, such as my duty in life, my avocations, my employment. Let all these things stay as they are, but what I am before Thee, my intellect, my will, my body, my soul, let all these be so changed that I may be not mine but Thine." Then we realize in the deepest sense, the words of St. Paul to the Galatians: "With Christ I hang upon the cross." We might put it into a prayer, saying: "I give myself to God, here is my body, take it. Here is my blood, take it. Here is my soul, my will, my energy, my strength, my property, my wealth—all that I have. It is Thine. Take it! Consecrate it! Offer it! Offer it with Thyself to the Heavenly Father in order that He, looking down on this great sacrifice, may see only Thee, His Beloved Son, in Whom He is well pleased. Transmute the poor bread of my life into Thy Divine Life; charge the wine of my wasted life with Thy Divine Spirit; unite my broken heart with Thy Heart; change my cross into a crucifix. Let not my abandonment, my sorrow, and my bereavement go to waste. Gather up the fragments and, as the drop of water is absorbed by the wine at the Offertory of the Mass, let my life be absorbed in Thine; let my little cross be entwined with Thy great Cross so that I may purchase the joys of everlasting happiness in union with Thee."

THE COMMUNION

In the Offertory, we are like lambs being led to the slaughter. In the Consecration, we are the lambs who are slaughtered in the lower part of our sinful selves. In the Communion, we find that we have not died at all but that we have come to life.

In order to understand by opposites what takes place in Holy Communion, consider the nature of a totalitarianism such as Communism. In such a philosophy of life, every person must surrender himself totally and completely, body and soul, mind and will, action and life, to a human dictator. In Christianity there is also a total surrender; we give ourselves completely and entirely to God through His Divine Son, Jesus Christ.

But here comes the great difference. In Communism those who deliver themselves over to the state are surrendering to materialism, for they are denying God and the soul. When one gives oneself up to that which is material, one becomes possessed by it, as a drowning man becomes possessed by the materiality of water, and a burning man becomes possessed by the materiality of fire, and a suffocated man becomes possessed by the materiality of earth. Communism can never enrich or exalt the souls of its followers.

But when there is a dedication to God, and when our death is to the lower part of ourselves as it is in the Consecration of the Mass, then we get back our souls ennobled and enriched. We begin at last to be free, glorified, divinized, exalted. We find that, after all, our death was no more permanent in the Consecration than was the death of Christ on Calvary, for in Holy Communion we surrender our humanity and we receive Divinity. We give up time and we get eternity, we give up our sin and we receive grace, we surrender our self-will and receive the omnipotence of Divine will. We give up petty loves and receive the Flame of Love, we give up our nothingness and we receive all. For Christ has said: "He . . . who loses his life for my sake . . . will save it."

There is another life above the life of the body; namely, the life of the soul. Just as the life of the body is the soul so, too, the life of the soul is God. This Divine life we receive in Communion. If the sunlight and moisture and the chemicals of the earth could speak they would say to the plants: "Unless you eat me you shall not have life in you;" if the plants and the herbs of the field could speak, they would say to the animals: "Unless you eat me you shall not have life in you;" if the animals and the plants and the chemicals of the universe could speak they would say to man: "Unless you eat me you shall not have life in you." So, too, the Son of God says to us that unless we receive of Him we shall not have Divine life in us. The law of transformation holds sway, the lower is transformed into the higher; chemicals into plants, plants into animals, animals into man and man into God without, however, man ever losing his personal identity. Hence the word that is used for Communion is "to receive" Our Lord, for literally we do receive the Divine life, more significantly than a babe receives human life as it is nursed by the mother, for in this latter case, the human is being nourished by the human, but in Communion the human receives Divine life from God. But like all words, even this one has some imperfection, for in communion it is not so much we who receive Christ as Christ who receives us, incorporating us into Himself.

We know we do not deserve this. All love really feels itself unworthy. The lover is always on his knees, the beloved always on a pedestal. Hence before receiving Communion we repeat with the priest: "*Domine non sum dignus*"—O, Lord, I am not worthy. It is as if we were holding ourselves back, conscious of the fact that we are unworthy of the Divine gift.

It is to be noted that there is no such thing as Communion without a sacrifice. Just as we cannot have the natural communion of eating, unless vegetables have been torn up from their roots and subjected to fire, and animals have been subjected to the knife and slain, and then submitted to purgation, so neither can we have Communion with Christ unless there is first a death. That is why the Mass is not just a Communion service; it is a sacrifice which ends in Communion. Communion is the consequence of Calvary; we live by what we slay. Our bodies live by the slaying of the beasts of the field and the plants of the garden; we draw life from their crucifixion; we slay them not to destroy but to have life more abundantly. We immolate them for the sake of communion.

By a beautiful paradox of Divine love, God makes His Cross the very means of our salvation and our life. We have slain Him; we have nailed Him there and crucified Him; but the Love in His eternal Heart could not be extinguished. He *willed* to give us the very life we slew; to give us the very Food we destroyed; to nourish us with the very Bread we buried, and the very Blood we poured forth. He made our very crime into a happy fault; He turned a Crucifixion into a Redemption; a Consecration into a Communion; a death into Life Everlasting.

And it is just this that makes man all the more mysterious! Why man should be loved is no mystery. But why he does not love in return is a great mystery. Why should Our Lord be the Great Unloved; why should Love not be loved? He is loved in all who unite themselves with Christ the Priest and the Victim.

Too long has the communion rail been as footlights dividing the stage of the altar from the audience. The Second Vatican Council has, as it were, broken down the "wall of division" and made the faithful living actors in the drama of Calvary. Because the faithful "die" with Christ in the Mass and "rise" with Him, the new liturgy restores the communion with Christ into a Christian community.

It is this drama of Redemption that M. Daniel-Rops has sought to clarify in this magnificent book in which he unites his profound knowledge of Christian tradition with the literary talents that have brought him the high honor of membership in the French Academy. M. Daniel-Rops' words have been complemented by the photographs of Mr. Yousuf Karsh, who has taken the mechanics out of photography and made it a fine art. The chapel which appears in the photographs is our own private chapel which was designed by our friend Leslie Dorsey, and the altar boy is our grandnephew, Francis Jerome Cunningham III. Literary and liturgical assistance of an invaluable kind was supplied by the Very Reverend Monsignor Edward T. O'Meara, S.T.D., Diocesan Director (in the Archdiocese of St. Louis) of the Society for the Propagation of the Faith. And the translation from the French by Mr. Alastair Guinan, as well as his useful notes, has preserved the full flavor of the original. It is Mr. Guinan, also, who has co-ordinated the changes which mark this new edition of *This is the Mass* so that, in text and in illustrative materials, it conforms to the Constitution on the Sacred Liturgy of the Second Vatican Council and to the most recent decrees of the Congregation of Rites and of the post-Conciliar Commission which serve to implement the provisions devised by the Council in the great work of responding to the pastoral needs of our own day.

MOST REVEREND FULTON J. SHEEN, D.D., Ph.D.
National Director of the Pontifical Society
for the Propagation of the Faith

Author's Preface

ONE OF THE POINTS most frequently emphasized, now-adays, in discussions of the Liturgy is the idea that the Mass (which repeats what was done by Our Lord at the Last Supper, the while *it offers to God,* as Trent put it, *a true and proper sacrifice*) is rooted in old Jewish rites. Such declarations lay great stress upon the Mass as being the fulfillment of the Passover Commemoration observed by devout Hebrews in the time of Christ, a rite traditionally preserved by rabbinical authorities in subsequent ages. It is very generally held that these ancient traditions have been carefully adhered to; but, in the absence of clear evidence, we cannot, with certainty, state *how exactly* this has been done. The Christian Scriptures rather imply (as in Luke 8:22) than expose the precise connection between the traditional Jewish rites and the actions and words of Our Lord at the Last Supper; but it is, in any event, important to remember that, as well as being the fulfillment of the Passover, the Mass is likewise its transformation; for it would scarcely be sound, either theologically or historically, to allow the emphasis which we justly lay upon what Christians share in common with the chosen people of old to obscure the distinctive features of the new Christian oblation which the author of the Epistle to the

Hebrews so tellingly contrasts with the oblations made aforetime in old Israel.[1] Nor ought we think that it has been reserved for our own age to discover identifying characteristics in Jewish Pasch and Christian Mass; for, seven hundred years ago, Aquinas sang:

> *Noctis recolitur coena novissima,*
> *Qua Christus creditur agnum et azyma*
> *Dedisse fratribus juxta legitima*
> *Priscis indulta patribus,*

the literal meaning of which is that Our Lord, at the Last Supper, gave to His brethren the lamb and the unleavened bread whose use was enjoined by the law given their fathers in former times. Thus did Aquinas testify to traditional belief. This Last Supper is, to Thomas, also *novissima*, the newest; for in Latin the word has this dual signification, and the idea of it seems to have been ever close to his mind: in the preceding stanza of the same hymn he had written:

> *Recedant vetera; nova sint omnia*
> (Let old things depart, let all things be new),

as if summing up the passing of the Old and the advent of the New Covenant, sealed by Christ in His own blood.[2] And, centuries earlier still, during the heyday of the great Carolingian liturgists, it was a fashion dear to scholars like Amalar to work out parallels, some well enough grounded, others reflecting no more than fancied allegorical analogy, between the sacred rites of Jewry, so splendidly carried out in the Temple during Old Testament times,[3] and the Christian liturgies. Always underlying this kind of devotional or scholarly writing, as well also as underlying officialdom's enactments and decrees, is to be perceived the concern which followers of Christ have consistently felt in their desire to carry out the divine injunction: "Do this in remembrance of Me." The liturgical codification of St. Gregory, the zeal with which Charlemagne strove to spread throughout Gaul the Roman Mass whose texts he had besought Pope Adrian to send him, the discerning care with which Alcuin adorned the rites of Adrian's Sacramentary,[4] the rigor with which the Tridentine Fathers and Pope Pius V prescribed a manner of celebrating the Latin rite Eucharist which clothed it in

uniformity, the enlightened interest which the bishops of seventeenth-
and eighteenth-century France showed in enriching the varied Mass-
books proper to their dioceses,[5] the pastoral solicitude of Pius X for the
active participation of worshipers in the liturgical life of the Church,
the concern for a right understanding of the theology of the liturgy
exemplified by Pius XII in his great Encyclical "Mediator Dei," and,
but yesterday, the reforms in the manner of liturgical worship which
the Fathers of the Second Vatican Council have determined upon—all
spring alike from a common conviction that the Mass is the essential
and characteristic function of the Church founded by Christ Our Lord,
and that the Church which *preaches Jesus Christ and Him crucified*
brings, everywhere, with it the Mass.

So it is that, every day, wherever the Cross has been set up,
Mass is said . . . In villages and in teeming cities, there is the Mass; in
the Far North or in some tropical hut, there is the Mass, as well. In the
early hours of morn, in some lonely church dotted here and there with
a few worshipers, Mass is said by a priest who seems to be functioning
for the sake of a mere handful of the devout; and, with high pomp,
amid a vast multitude gathered in the brilliantly lighted Basilica of St.
Peter, Mass is said after the Vicar of Christ has been borne on the *Sedia
Gestatoria* before the Altar to the sound of joyous acclamation. Times
unnumbered, and at every moment of the day, Mass is said in one or
another place throughout the world. The late Pius XII, in his Encyclical
"Mediator Dei," calls the Mass "the chief act of divine worship, the
apex and the core of the Christian religion;"[6] and the Second Vatican
Council, in its Constitution on the Sacred Liturgy, terms the Mass,
instituted by Our Saviour, "a memorial of His death and resurrection, a
sacrament of love, a sign of unity, a bond of charity, a paschal banquet
in which Christ is received: the mind is filled with grace, and an earnest
of future glory is given to us."[7]

Yet what does this act mean to us who assist at the culmination
of the worship man wishes to offer to God, to us who through it come
face to face with the essence and the core of our faith, to us who attend
Mass; and what does it make of us? A young man of our day who was
seeking for something in which he might believe cried out: "These
people come down from Golgotha, and then they talk about the

weather!" It is to a great act of immolation that we have been called, to the commemoration of an act of sacrifice which is all the more unexampled in that the victim is at once willing to suffer and nevertheless wholly innocent of wrong-doing. We are here confronted with the unfathomed mystery of the ransoming blood of that spotless victim of sin, in whose weakness is perfect strength and in whose life death dies. Were it not that thoughtlessness and heedless familiarity lie over our souls like a hard crust, we could not bear to come to Mass as though it were but some conventionalism of social ceremony; for we would realize that it should mean everything to us, and that in face of it providing Love's answer to Faith's most tantalizing and contradictory problems, we might well feel our minds struck dumb, our sensibilities deeply touched, and our hearts themselves wholly subdued by love.

The meaningful core of the Mass lies in this, that it is *par excellence* a drama which is ceaselessly enacted before us, a tragedy everlastingly prolonged. The name by which this drama has been known since the sixth century is a term taken from the formulary with which, aforetime, it was brought to its closure—the formulary, *Ite Missa est*—and it seems all too curt a word wherewith to clothe so ineffable a mystery. It seems, indeed, that other names for the Mass which were once in use, are more suitable—Thanksgiving; Liturgy; the Breaking of Bread; Synaxis, or assembly; or, to follow the usage of Tertullian, Justin Martyr, and St. Cyprian of Carthage, we might call it *Dominica Passio*, the Passion of the Lord. Herein lies the truth, for it is the Passion of Christ which inspires the Mass, that Passion besought, declared, manifested, and fulfilled. Everything in the Mass converges on this fundamental fact of Christian faith, that our Redemption was wrought by the sacrifice of the Cross; and it is in relation to it rather than to a simple formulary of dismissal that the Mass is best understood.

Basically, the Mass preserves, in precise terms, the memory of that Last Supper at which Jesus, but a short time before He suffered and died, blessed the bread and the wine and made of them His body and His blood, and then said: "Do this for a commemoration of Me" (Luke 22:19). His pregnant words, effecting by transubstantiation the change of two very ordinary earthly substances into supernatural substances, are the vehicles of a two-fold message. By them was foretold the death of Christ in willing offering of Himself, even before the enemies of Jesus became the ministrants at His oblation: "So", says St. Paul, "so it is the Lord's death that you are heralding, whenever you eat this bread, and drink this cup, until he comes" (I Cor. 11:26). And, by the same token, inasmuch as He offered to His disciples the bread and the wine which had been so marvelously changed, He made them sharers at another Table as well as at that Last Supper; that is to say, at the Table of everlasting life. Therefore, the Mass is a remembrance of three truths: it is the re-enactment of the words and gestures which marked the consecration that took place at the Last Supper; it is the lively memorial, charged with its own dramatic meaning, of the sacrifice offered on Calvary's hill; it is the banquet-table to which all the baptized are called.

Historically, the kernel of the Mass lies in its being a presentment of the Last Supper through the repetition of those words and acts there taught us by Christ, words and acts whose fathomless significance the faith of the first Christians knew how to apprehend. So it is that there may be pictured those early Masses which the Apostles celebrated after the Ascension Day or after the first Pentecost. They were quite simple, and indeed they consisted of no more than the careful repetition of what the Apostles had been taught. This note of an austere simplicity endured throughout the whole apostolic age. Do we not see St. Paul, while on one of his missionary journeys, officiating at "the breaking of bread" in a simple room on the third floor of a dwelling house while surrounded by a group which the little room could scarcely contain? (Acts 20:7 sqq). This sacred Supper was not separated from the Agapé or Love Feast in which the primitive Christians gathered together that they might bind themselves to fellowship in the Lord.

After the passing of almost twenty centuries, the Mass has lost the note of stark austerity. Other elements have been superimposed on the fundamental evangelical structure. The chief of these are a direct inheritance from the divine service of the older dispensation. Were not the Apostles children of Moses? Were they not convinced that they were showing their fidelity to the precepts of his law when they gave adhesion to the Revelation of Christ? As the Gospels and the Book of the Acts testify, divine service in the Jewish synagogues was made up of two parts. The *prayer service* comprised the singing or recitation of prayers from the Scriptures, especially from one or another of those wonderful passages in the Book of Psalms wherein human fervency pours itself out in a fashion elsewhere unsurpassed. The *didactic service* consisted in listening to readers who took up the holy books of the Law and the Prophets. These characteristic notes were maintained in Christian services of worship; and even when Christians had entirely discontinued participation in the Jewish worship, they retained its chief features in their own. In this lies the root of the prayers at the beginning of Mass and of the readings from the Epistles and the Gospels.

The Mass became set much as we now know it, insofar as concerns its broad structure, at about the close of the third century. Although this or that part may show some growth or some diminution in importance from the usages of that time, the general plan of the ceremony is even now just such as it was then. However, in primitive times the details of the Mass were not as rigorously fixed as they are in our day, and apart from an adherence to basic matters, there was a degree of permissible latitude which allowed the bishop, or even the celebrating priest, to express himself in extemporaneous prayer. Notable divergencies in the manner of celebrating Mass long flourished, as can easily be seen by taking up and comparing some of the old *Sacramentaries,* those Missals so magnificently written and painted which were in use at solemn ceremonials during the whole period of the high Middle Ages. Even in our own time, one may find certain differences in Rite or Use attached, by privilege, to particular dioceses (Lyon and Milan are two examples) or to religious orders (as the Carthusians, Dominicans, or Premonstratensians). Above all is this distinction to be perceived in the sumptuous and prolix Liturgies of the East when these are contrasted with the relatively simple Rites of the West in our day.

During the course of the centuries, certain new elements have been received into the Mass according to the living tradition of the Church; and just as the more elaborate music which succeeded the graver measures of the old plainchant clearly gives evidence of freedom from the restraints imposed on the more primitive constituents of the old liturgy, all these newer elements possess in common two characteristics: they interrupt the course of the eucharistic prayer, and they often display great subjectivity and individualism. The *Gloria,* for example, was originally an acclamatory hymn proper to the Midnight Mass of Christmas when it gave voice to the joy of Christian hearts in commemorating the Redeemer's birth; while the *Credo,* to cite another instance, is an individualistic proclamation of personal faith and belief which found a place in the Mass at about the year 1000, being then most probably introduced to repel heretical doubt. Certain acts which to us would appear to be of manifest necessity in the Mass, such as the *Great Elevation,* are likewise later additions to its primitive structure. In this instance, the solemn showing of the Host to the people serves as a reply to the separatist's contention that God is not present in the Eucharistic Elements. There is something attractively persuasive in the traditional adornments thus added to the framework of the Mass: they prove, indeed, the living heritage of a faith which ceaselessly re-states itself.

The generally rigidly regulated form of the Western Mass (which had marked it for the all but four centuries antecedent to the Second Vatican Council) was fixed on the morrow of the Council of Trent by St. Pius V. By his Bull "Quo primum" of 1570, he expressed a wish to recall the Mass to its antique norms; he attempted at once to disencumber it of certain incidental elements and to impose its observance in uniform fashion throughout Latin Christendom. The Mass was thus given definitive form by being closely associated with the Primacy of the Apostolic See and the authority of St. Peter's successor, while the Mass Book endorsed by the Tridentine Fathers was none other than that used in the Eternal City, the *Roman Missal.*

Therefore was it declared in the Catechism of the Council of Trent that no part of that Missal ought be considered *vain or superfluous;* that not even the least of its phrases is to be thought wanting or insignificant. The shortest of its formularies, phrases even which take no more than a few seconds to pronounce, form integral parts of a whole wherein are drawn together and set forth God's gift, Christ's sacrifice, and the grace which is dowered upon us. This whole conception has in view a sort of spiritual symphony in which all themes are taken as being expressed, developed, and unified under the guidance of one purpose. It is a spiritual symphony, however, directed by the teaching authority of the Church which, without altering the essentials of the divine institution, can and does change details. Thus, as recently as 1956; the late Pope Pius XII declared in his Allocution to the members of the First International Congress of Pastoral Liturgy, "There are found in the liturgy unchangeable elements, a sacred content which transcends time; but there are, as well, elements which are variable and transitory,— sometimes even imperfect."[8]

Our own generation is the witness of certain much-publicized changes in this Roman liturgy, changes founded on the initiative toward reform of the Mass rite given by the Council and on the effort to realize this reform made by the Congregation of Sacred Rites and the post-Conciliar Commission in Rome and by local Liturgical Commissions acting in the name of the bishops of various dioceses, in conjunction with territorial or national commissions. There has been an understandable tendency toward exaggerating the nature and the extent of this reform on the part of publicists, polemicists, and partisans of this or that notion of what it is most desirable to strive after in recasting the venerable forms of our worship. Basically, the Mass is to remain what it always has been; the changes are designed not to revolutionize its content but to make that content more readily comprehensible to the man of the day. Not a few of these changes are presented as seeking to express the outcome of a more critical experience, on the part of those whose office it is to feed the flock of Christ, of the deeply tragic contrariousness seated in the heart of modern man. Hence the simplification, by either curtailment or excision, of certain elements evolved during a more leisurely and gracious time than is our own harried period in history; hence the concession, where local authority deems it opportune, to allow an increased use of vernacular formularies within the course of the liturgical action in order that the congregation, in general, may be made to feel more at ease with prayers and gestures which, in the ideal sense, are to be taken as being representative of the attitude and response of every member of that congregation.[9] It is with the hope of increasing the sense and reality of personal involvement in what is going on within the sanctuary that we now find in many parish churches the revival of such long-forgotten features of worship as an altar over which the celebrating priest faces the people; [10] a more sharply defined division of *synaxis* and *anaphora,* now termed, respectively, the Liturgy of the Word and the Liturgy of the Eucharist; the omission of prayers like the *Judica me* and the *Last Gospel,* which are, from the viewpoint of the historian, late additions to the service; the reintroduction of antique ritual gestures and formularies, or the abandonment of others which came into use only after the first millennium of Christianity had come to its term; the proclamation, in the vernacular, by the Celebrant in Low Masses, and by either himself or by one of the sacred ministers in Sung Masses, of the Gospel pericope proper to the Office of the Mass which is being sung or said (a text which modern congregations had grown accustomed to hearing so read from the pulpit before the Sermon, rather than at the point at which it actually occurs in the rite); the insistence on the maintenance of the homiletic character of the sermon in order that it may be attached firmly to the underlying thought of the day's assigned Scripture readings; [11] the revival, where the local Ordinary judges it expedient, of the old litanic general intercession, *a prayer for all sorts and conditions of men,* which the recent decrees allow "competent territorial authority" to reintroduce under the name of the *Common Prayer* or the *Prayer of the Faithful;* [12] and, lastly, the relaxation, for Christmas and Easter, of the long-standing regulation which permitted lay communicants to approach the Holy Table only once within each twenty-four-hour day. [13]

No Catholic who has had, hitherto, a right understanding of what the Mass really is will see in any of these changes a true or substantial alteration in the essential nature of the Mass: the changes affect its peripheral shell. The determination of what actions, formularies, gestures constitute the liturgical worship which has slowly, for centuries, grown up around the sacred Words of Institution enshrined within the Canon, rests with the supreme teaching authority of the Church, as presently manifested in the document on the Liturgy approved ("almost unanimously," as His Holiness Pope Paul has said) by the Council, and then promulgated by the Holy See; it is not a matter of individual preference or personal predilection. The possibility of just such a conflict, as is suggested by the juxtaposition here of the two notions, *authoritative deci-*

sion and *individual preference,* had already been foreseen by the late Sovereign Pontiff, Pius XII, when he mordantly remarked, in 1956, that, in reaction to such changes as are here envisioned, there "is manifested the diversity of temperaments as well as preferences favoring either individual piety or community worship." He had just previously noted that "the faithful adopt profoundly different attitudes in responding to the measures taken by the Church; some," as he remarked, "will show readiness, enthusiasm, occasionally even a too active desire which demands the intervention of authority; others will show indifference and even opposition." [14] These words prompt the student of ecclesiastical history to the reflection, no less valid at this period in the progress of the Church than it is in respect to certain crises and conflicts in the past, that the right of the teaching authority of the Church to regulate affairs of this kind is truly a matter of dogma, but the question of how far that right has been exercised wisely and how far unwisely is certainly a matter of history. The latter question may, therefore, confidently be left to historians; for those who concern themselves with such delicate problems and their even more difficult solutions will, indubitably, have much to say to us in the not distant future, allowance being made for a reasonable period of experimentation and assessment. At this point, we may, therefore, profitably return to our consideration of the essential nature of the Mass, insofar as that is revealed by the appearance or plan which enshrouds this sublime reality of the Christian life.

What then is the plan of the Mass? Its traditional division into the Mass of the Catechumens and the Mass of the Faithful—in the terminology of the day, the Liturgy of the Word, and the Liturgy of the Eucharist—is the result of historical circumstances; for the first part owes its existence to a provision for admitting to the common worship of Christians the unbaptized neophytes as well as the baptized, while the Mass of the Faithful is so called because, after a certain point in the service had been reached, the unbaptized were, in olden days, dismissed. But it is the very manner of development assumed by the liturgy, it is the arc of its fulfillment, which best marks out the moments or "acts" of the Mass in the very sense in which that term is used in respect of the drama. There are five such acts. In the first of them when I am on the threshold of this sacramental action, I *pray:* I beg that God will forgive what I have done amiss; I speak to Him of my will to know Him; I raise my voice in praise and in supplication. In the second, I *hear* the teaching of the Church, first as that teaching has been received from the Apostles or was prophetically declared in the inspired books of the Old Law, and later in the words of Jesus Himself in the Gospel. The substance of this teaching is summed up in the *Credo* which I then repeat by way of affirming my assent to it. Next, I find myself entering upon the sacrificial liturgy properly so considered. Christ Himself offers Himself in an oblation which is the sacramental core of the Mass, and it is my privilege to join in this grace-giving act. I therefore *offer*, through the ministration of the priestly celebrant who is at once my witness and my representative, I *offer* those fruits of the earth which are to be changed; and this offering is, in itself, symbolic of that more personal, and wholly interior oblation, which I make of myself, so that offering and offerer become one. The fourth division is the most profound in meaning: it comprises the *sacrificial act* itself by which and in which the victim is immolated. It is I myself who by intimate participation in the sacrificial action of the priest, it is I myself who effect this immolation in which the victim of the *sacrifice* and its ministrant are one: again the divine Body is nailed to the Cross; again the redeeming Blood gushes forth. And, finally, in obedience to the will of Christ, I *receive* the Holy Communion and am nourished at the Table of everlasting life.

So it is that, step by step, the liturgy of the Mass unfolds itself before our eyes in an impressive harmony which allows of no comparison. In it and by it is every aspect of man's religion duly accomplished: the Mass is the summation and complement of all man's hopes and good purposes. The Mass is the implementation of an interchange between God and myself: by it all that I would seek in my prayer is gradually brought to fulfillment almost before I have put my desire into words. Yet it may be asked if its effect is something which concerns nothing more than the relations existing between God and myself? It is true, indeed, that by the first of the new commandments we are enjoined to love God with our whole mind and heart; but it must not be overlooked that the second which is, as we have been taught, *like unto the first,* requires that man love his neighbor as himself. He has not understood the Mass at all who has failed to perceive that by it these two commandments are unceasingly recalled to our remembrance.

The Mass first came into being as an act of common prayer: it was the prayer of the re-united Twelve, the prayer of those early Christian believers who were so bound in devotion one to another that they shared their goods in common, it was the prayer of the Martyrs who mingled their blood in a common confession of the One Lord. It is no more than the simple truth to declare that at Mass we are all but little cells in one body, each of us a sheep that belongs to the one fold. The most outstandingly beautiful prayers of the liturgy—and they are among the most ancient as well—the *Collects*, the *Secrets*, and the *Postcommunions*, are not grasped in their true significance unless they be considered as expressing *the common prayer*. They teach a lesson which is re-stated by the *Mementos*—one of the living, the other of the dead—which we find inserted in the prayer of the Consecration itself: beyond all claims of time and space, beyond the all-compelling exactions of death itself, we make ourselves ready for union with God in just the degree that we are joined in fellowship one with another; and this is the whole sense and burden of the Communion of Saints.

For the Mass is born of a two-fold meaning and purpose. It is my own most urgent concern: herein lie my life and my death. It is for me, all unworthy as I am, it is for me that every Mass is celebrated: *"for you it is that there gushes forth this drop of My Blood . . ."* Yet, the fullest meaning of the Mass is unrealized unless it be shared in fellowship by me with all the children of God, unless they somehow join me in the path that leads to the Light, for *the soul when lifted up, shall draw the world unto it;* and each one of us is charged with the welfare of all. It is, of course, only the whole Church, considered from its very beginnings as extending and enduring until the end of time, that is worthy and able to gather the elements and to set forth the oblation in this sacrifice to the Infinite God. The Mass is our own concern: it concerns every one of us. And it is as one individual, however insignificant, in the great multitude of human souls for whom Christ thirsted and whom He has redeemed in His own Blood, it is as one individual united to all my fellows by faith and in hope, that I now will to assist at Mass the while my heart is bowed in love and in expectation of the coming of the Lord.

This is the Mass

Prelude

It is a natural impulse, enforced by reasoned reflection, which suggests the fittingness of a moment of preparation prior to any deed of importance: hence it is especially suitable that some time of recollection precede our participation in the Mass. The Code of Canon Law explicitly enjoins upon priests the duty of preparing themselves for the celebration of Mass by prayer said beforehand;[1] while the Roman Missal provides a whole series of psalms, collects, and other prayers from which they are urged to make at least a selection. Moreover, the series of prayers which have, ever since the late sixteenth century, stood at the beginning of the *Ordo Missae* or Ordinary of the Mass are formularies which evolved out of the private prayers of preparation used by the celebrating priest on his way to the altar, as a personal act of approach to the Holy mysteries.[2] Standing on the threshold of the Mass, he said, *"Introïbo,"* while leaving the sacristy; and it was only with the passing of time that these prayers came to be said within the sanctuary itself, despite the fact that they still kept a certain tone about them befitting private prayer. Historically, therefore, they represent a late addition to the Mass, a fact which explains the disposition of them made by the newest decrees of the Congregation of Rites and of the post-Conciliar Commission.[3] Their first appearance dates only from the seventh century, and they did not come into general usage until 1570, when Pius V made the Roman Missal obligatory. The words of these prayers are meaningful; and Psalm 42 recalls the exiled Jews grieving by the waters of Babylon. They wept for their despoiled altar, for their abandoned Holy Place. But these words testify, too, to a faith which stands unshaken, to an entire trust in God. As the verses of this Psalm succeed each other, it is hope that outrings sorrow. For this reason, in the early Church—at Milan, for example, in the days of St. Ambrose—the newly baptized sang this psalm on Easter Eve, when they were first admitted to a full share in the Mass. In our own day, recent changes in the outward form of the Liturgy of the Mass provide that certain passages in these prayers be omitted, as was indeed previously the case, according to the Tridentine Missal, in respect to Masses in Passiontide, Funeral Masses, and other services for the dead.[4] Although Psalm 42, the beautiful *Judica me*, is no longer said by the celebrant before the altar, it may still, quite properly, form part of our private preparation.

I AM COME, my Lord, in a ready spirit, armed with hope and with love. I look on this Mass as a happy oasis in my life, as a source of refreshment and of vigor, so that with a right heart I may resume my work; so that the burdens which, oft-times, I find beyond bearing may be lightened through Your loving kindness and Your indulgent aid.

How many are the hours I spend without a thought of You, my God; forgetful even of my own soul, but in the grip of alien forces! Keep me mindful of You, and of what I am to You: for to think of one is to think of the other. I pray that these moments which are made holy by being passed in Your Presence, may be a source of faith, of fervor, and of joy.

Take away from me this bitterness which throttles me, this harsh and agonizing dryness which holds me in its grip, this darksome discouragement which broods around me. Cleanse me from secret leanings to sin, from inclinations impelling me to choose what is unworthy, from all the evil that I would not and that I yet do. At the very beginning of this Mass, make me ready to be what You would have me be.

I

Introïbo
ad Altare Dei

THE PRAYERS AT THE FOOT OF THE ALTAR

After he has made the sign of the Cross, and before he recites the *Confiteor,* the priest says words which summarize his feelings on entering the sanctuary of the Most High God: "I will go up to the altar of God, to God, the giver of triumphant happiness." How apparent and how meaningful do these words of Scripture become as we think of them in the light cast on them by thought of a rebirth, a restoration, of youthful fervor; for it is with a youthful heart, in a spirit overflowing with joy, that we should come before the living God Who has chosen to abide with us, always living upon our altars to make intercession for us before the Face of the Father. The priest, who is our representative, thus voices the sentiments which

fill the heart of the faithful Christian who knows that he is on his way to that altar of sacrifice whence he is to draw a new draught of life and spiritual energy. It is in the Holy Communion, by which we shall mark our fullest participation in this Mass, that we receive from God an earnest of eternal life, which is the true everlasting youth. Elsewhere in the Church's liturgy, the Holy Eucharist is referred to as a pledge or earnest of future glory; [1] and it is the common teaching of theologians that in the beatific state the bodies of the glorified just will be restored to their primal state of perfection. It is in anticipation of all this that the soul, having passed over the threshold of the Mass, feels itself vested in joy.

O GOD, my trust in You is boundless. My first word is one of entire confidence in You. I believe in You; in You do I place my trust: it is You alone who are the rock of my being and the fulcrum of my strength. And it is because I am no more in Your sight than a reed, a reed which rests in Your hands, that I know myself to be strong.

Therefore am I glad, glad in my Lord. There awaits me a renewal of my forces, in which my soul shall come to full growth. By the glad light of this confrontation with You for which I now make ready, my Lord, I beg You to lead me henceforth along the way in which I should go. Guide me by Truth, which is the right hand of Your Love.

II

Confiteor

THE GENERAL CONFESSION OF SINS

In the very instant of its surrender to joy, the soul is held back by a heaviness within itself, as a wall of separation looms between the soul and God. This vexing obstacle is the soul's knowledge of its own sinfulness. In the primitive Church, which had its roots in the heart of Christ, there was a spontaneous sense of the soul's need to ask for pardon at the beginning of Mass. (And, indeed, it seems that there may have then existed a penitential rite like the washing of the disciples' feet by Jesus before the Last Supper.) Little by little, there came into usage the formal declaration of the soul's sinful state and an accompanying plea for pardon. In the eighth and ninth centuries, under the title of *Apologia,* devout souls began to compose *excusatory prayers* in which pleading mingled with confession. The Roman Missal as drawn up in 1570 preserves one of these formularies constructed in the dramatic manner associated with the four stages of a trial: the soul appears before the bar of justice, the soul confesses its guilt, the advocates plead, and pardon is granted. This is a public collective prayer in which priest and people antiphonally acknowledge their sinfulness, not just privately, but in the face of the whole Church, of all her saintly witnesses, and even in the face of the very powers of Heaven.

Thus does the *Confiteor* strike, initially, that note of the sense of fellowship, of communion one with another, which marks Mass-goers.

The thrice repeated act of deep repentance, at *mea culpa,* when the hand strikes the breast in an old biblical and monastic gesture, brings consolation to the sinner in his racking sorrow; for is it not written that the prayer of the humble shall be heard before the Most High? (Ecclus. 35:21).

ALL HEAVEN is listening, all the great saints of the past: I am in the presence not alone of Him before whose gaze nothing lies hid, not alone of that strange and penetrating discernment which belongs to God's angels, but as well in the sight of every man and woman strong enough to have lived by love, of every saint and martyr whose mere existence is a condemnation of my own sinfulness.

What shall I, a sinner, now be saying as against me rises the voice of the accuser, the voice that brings me sharply to account? The knowledge that I am guilty suffices to stop my own voice; it forbids my attempt at any defence.

Against me stand my own actions which, even though human justice might not deem them worthy of reproof, I know to be in some sense wanting or even worse. My secret thoughts rise up from those shoals of wretchedness and dejection which the self-satisfied sloth of human complacency serves but to conceal. And I am faced, too, with all that I have left undone, with my failures, with my back-slidings and strayings, with all the overwhelming burden of my unspoken assents to wrong.

I would that the thrice-repeated gesture of penitence, made upon my breast, might bestir my heart and awaken my soul from the torpor of its heavy sleep, by recalling me to all that I should do.

Now all around me are also the mysterious forces of loving kindness. All these saints of past times, all the powers of Heaven, serving as a tribunal of accusation and judgment, are become my intercessors before the Infinite One. The Virgin's purity, the martyrs' blood, the shining forbearance of the saints, are become my safeguard in the mysterious economy of the sharing of merit through the Communion of Saints.

And while the words of absolution resound, I cast aside thought of my fear that I shall fall again tomorrow and have to start over once more, and I stand upright in joy regained as, suddenly, I sense an indescribable relief.

III

The Kissing of the Altar

THE PRIEST GOES UP TO THE HOLY TABLE

The prayers at the foot of the altar were but an introduction; the priest now goes up, step by step, to the altar. Using some words from that Psalm (84: *Benedixisti Domine*) which is so associated with the joys of Christmastide, he has first prayed that God would show His face to His people in order that in Him they may find their joy. But at the very moment of his beginning to go up the steps a shadow falls over the heart of the priest and, in the words of an old prayer which was already in use in Rome in the fifth century (*Aufer a nobis, quaesumus, Domine, iniquitates nostras . . .*), he implores the Lord to cleanse the soul desirous of penetrating to the holy place.

Now the priest stands before the altar, before the most holy object which the church contains, before that altar which is its center and its apex, an object of a mysterious meaningfulness which can never be fully fathomed. A symbol of Christ, is not the altar also the place which serves to table the Body and Blood of the Crucified? And is it not also, as St. Ambrose tells us, the very type of

that holy Body itself, for on the day the altar was consecrated it received the unction proper to the Lord's Anointed when it was annealed with the Sacred Chrism? [1] The five crosses which are cut into the stone recall Our Lord's five wounds. The altar also represents the Church: the relics of her saints are encased within the table, and the priest who is come to celebrate the Sacrifice does so in the Church's name. In the presence of the awesome sense of glory which emanates from the altar, the priest, in devout veneration, touches that holy table with his lips. Now by this kiss he signifies the union typified by the kiss which the Spouse gives to His Bride. And indeed, what the priest is proposing to accomplish here is nothing other than to forge the union of the Church to her Master, of the soul to its Redeemer.

It is this same excess of joy which causes the priest thus to salute the altar that we feel rising up within us in our moments of deepest inspiration. Then it is that we dress that altar of our souls, that altar whereon Christ desires to rest.

50

As YOUR ALTAR, my Lord, stands in the very heart of this church, visible to all by being set in that highest place where spiritual truth rises to fitting eminence, grant that, in my own heart, concern for You may take the highest place in the very core and apex of my being.

As this tabernacle shelters Your living presence which with fullest faith I now confess, grant that my soul may learn to know You, whom no man calls to account; and that you may become nearer to me than is my innermost thought.

As in this holy table are enclosed the memorials of a cloud of witnesses, the holy relics of Your saints, our pledges of everlasting life, grant that I may fully appreciate my place in Your Church, and that my soul may cleave to You in the Church.

As the priest now devoutly bows before Your altar, awed by its sacramental glory, grant me to know my own littleness and Your greatness; grant me so to subdue and trample under earthly pride that I may seek and find fulfillment, not in my own poor vanity, but in Him who alone endures.

Finally, as this kissing of the altar is an avowal and an earnest of that love before which the delights of all earthly loves languish and pale, grant, Lord Jesus, that I may love You, that I may more fully know You, that I may do only what You will as I bow before the secret altar which is set within my soul.

IV

The Introït

THE ENTRANCE VERSICLE

According to the manner of saying Mass set forth in the Tridentine Missal with which we are all familiar, the priest, after having kissed the altar, used to go to the right side of the holy table to read the *Introït* from the book which had been set there. The new *Ordo Missae* of 1965 offers alternate modes of its recitation in order to emphasize more dramatically the separation of the synaxis or Liturgy of the Word from the anaphora, the Eucharistic Liturgy, which will follow it. Nowadays, the celebrant is free to read this prayer either from the accustomed end of the altar, from the ambo or lectern, or from the place where his seat is set.[1] At High Mass, when the choir sings the *Introït*, or if the congregation recite it at Low Mass, the priest no longer reads it at all. The formulary is called the *Introït* because it was the old Entrance Chant—the *Ingressa* (or going-in verse), as it is called in the Ambrosian Liturgy. Its meaning becomes clear only in the light of an understanding of the old ceremonial of which these few words are the only surviving memorial. In the early days of the Roman Church, the Pope went from the Lateran Palace in most solemn cortege to the particular sanctuary in which Mass was, that day, to be said. This rite existed in the fifth century under St. Celestine V, and it

was later embellished and amplified by St. Gregory the Great. In it lies the origin of the processional entrance. Psalms were chanted by alternating choirs—in antiphonal style, as it is called—psalms which were specially chosen for their consonance with the underlying intention of the particular day's sacrifice. Thus they were joyous in Advent, but mournful in Lent. On saints' days they hymned their glorious triumph, and when the Epiphany and the Transfiguration were being commemorated their theme was the royalty of Christ. Thus the *Introït* became an entrance-song or introduction in a two-fold sense. In our time, there is but a vestige of this impressive rite in the use of a single anthem followed by a psalm verse (or, on occasion, of a passage from some other book of Scripture), with *Gloria Patri* and the repetition of the anthem.[2] Nevertheless, even this foreshortened, elliptical *Introït* keeps its function, differing as it does from day to day and serving always as a sort of spiritual introduction which, by a few brief words, states the theme or point of emphasis of the Mass formulary which it opens. According to the rubrics currently in force, the celebrating priest no longer makes the sign of the Cross on those occasions when he does read the *Introït*.[3]

MY LORD, as You once spoke to the heart of the great St. Augustine through the voice of the Psalms, You now speak to me in the words which the Church has appointed for today's *Introït*. Grant that, like Your servant Augustine, I, too, may allow these sounds to flow into my ears as a means by which the truth may penetrate my heart and there enkindle my devotion to You.

May I begin, today, to respond more fully to the promptings of that inner and lasting light which devotion brings to birth in my heart, and by which You guide me.

May I learn, through Your Voice, all that is truly for my good; for it is impossible to know these things, in their fullness, when I am estranged from You.

As I hear the words chosen by Your Church from the inspired writings of the Psalter, may I know that in You alone is my peace, and that I shall know peace only when I am united to Your Will.[4]

V

The Mercy and the Glory of God

THE KYRIE AND THE GLORIA

Two thematic notions recur again and again in the Mass: we here find them brought together in two prayers which are complementary each to the other, the *Kyrie* and the *Gloria*. To give glory to God and to beg His mercy are the two purposes which link man to God: it is because we know that God is Almighty that we beseech Him to have mercy upon us. And are not all the varying nuances of these inseparable purposes tellingly expressed in the words of the beautiful prayers to which the Church has given place at this point in liturgical worship? They are prayers which serve wondrously to sum up our yearning for divine things the while, by increasing our fervency, they bespeak our hope of salvation.

The *Kyrie* is a remnant of those litanic dialogues, of those acclamatory prayers, which rose up spontaneously in the breast of the primitive Church. It originated in the Greek-speaking East, perhaps in Jerusalem where the Spanish pilgrim, Etheria,[1] heard it sung about the year 500; and it is in Greek that we still say it. After the opening of the ceremony by the *Introït* with its three verses from Holy Writ, this simple plea carries, to the Three Divine Persons in turn, our heartfelt need and purposive desire for salvation.

Then, at once, there is intoned a hymn to the Majesty of God. The *Gloria* is a very old prayer, already in existence in the second century, which was incorporated into the Roman Mass in the sixth century.[2] It opens appropriately with the words in which the angels sang praise "to God in the highest"; for is not every Mass a renewal, in some sense, of Christmas, and does it not mark, once more, the Coming of Our Lord? Beginning with this Gospel verse, the ages of faith launch into a hymn of praise which, in its free-flowing fulsomeness, is like a torrent of love unleashed.

Yet even this emphasis on the Father's glory cannot conceal from man his own wretched state.

For this reason, when address is made to Christ our Mediator, the hymn re-echoes the appeal for mercy voiced by the *Kyrie:* it is because He is holy, because He is the Lord, because He is the Most High God, that Jesus brings us salvation.

And it is in suggesting the shining reflection of the bright glory of Father, Son, and Holy Spirit, which is itself the pledge of salvation in a believer's soul, that this most beautiful of hymns is brought to its end in sublime simplicity.

58

NOW THAT, three times, the three-fold petition has been raised to You, and has come from the depths of the souls of all Your creatures throughout all ages as a cry of hope, as a petition for pardon;

now that the angelic choirs and the unforgotten voices of all our brethren in the Faith have acclaimed Your glory, and have given thanks for the Name of Your glory;

grant, my Lord, that my healed spirit may be established before You in quietude, so that I may enter even into Your presence and there cry out to You in plain words: "My God, I love You; it is You that I worship; my God, show mercy to me"—for having said this, I shall have said all.

VI

Made One in the Lord

THE COLLECT

It is not enough to have adored and to have asked for mercy: a sense of unity is part of every Mass. *"Dominus vobiscum,"* cries out the priest—"the Lord be with you"—as with extended arms he turns to face the people.[1] And it would appear that the Liturgy seeks by means of this action, by the employment of this old salutation borrowed from Biblical usage, to satisfy a wish that all the faithful may be gathered together and made one in their supplication. This action is repeated at eight solemn times during the Mass: it is just such a gathering together of suppliants as it bespeaks that inspires the prayers called *Collects* which now follow. They are grave as Latin inscriptions in their terms and seem as if incised upon medals.

This is one of the chief moments of prayer at Mass, the other times being signalized by the Prayer over the *Oblations*[2] and the *Post-communion* prayers. These prayers are addressed to the Trinity in Unity; and, while the people stand,[3] the priest with hands extended reads them from the book. Should he have to pronounce the name of Jesus, he bows his head.[4] Is it because these prayers sum up and gather together all the intentions of the day's sacrifice, that they are called *Collects*? Historically that title recalls the old custom of Urban Rome where, about the fourth century, it was the practice for the whole Christian community to come together in one church that they might proceed with solemnity to the sanctuary chosen for the celebration of the day's Mass: in this sense the Collect is the prayer of the *plebs collecta*, the prayer of the assembled people. Were those Christians of the Middle Ages then so much at fault when they pushed this term further, and explained the word as meaning the *common prayer*? As he recites these prayers, is not the priest gathering together, as if in one sheaf, all our hopes and all our good purposes as if to offer them to God?[5] And, once more, is not the kiss with which the celebrant again salutes the altar before saying these prayers, is not the kiss a sign of the uniting of the assembly in Christ?

LORD, it is not for myself alone I now do pray,
   for selfish prayer is scarce a prayer at all;
But for all these, Your people, seen and unseen, for
   those who bear Your blessèd Sign, for these I pray;
Nor do I now forget those others who know You not,
   or who, knowing, have forsaken Your way:
For all we are one in You.

With all these, then, I join in that appointed invocation
   which Your church does place upon our lips today;
For to each day is given its own singular fashion
   wherewith to praise You and to pray to You;
That praying thus our lasting wish may come to be
   and we may grasp that which alone abides.

From an undivided heart, and in child-like spirit,
   to all these prayers I do myself unite,
As Your church in due humility does now pour out
   in words of plain and forceful sense,
Mankind's fear of oppression, famine, evil deeds,
   and its need of the dew of Your Love.

Thus guided by the saints whom we do now recall,
   be they close or distant, familiar or scarce known,
I join the age-long cloud of witnesses
   in ranks unbroken and unceasing,
While with these lips You've given me, I frame the Church's prayer
   and strive to reach the foot of Your Eternal Throne.

VII

The Reading in God's Name

THE EPISTLE

The *Amen* which concludes the *Collects* brings to its end the first part of the Ante-Mass. To that act of religion called *prayer,* there now succeeds another act of religion—that of *listening* to the Word. "I have a message . . . from the Lord," we are told by the Bible (Judges 3:20); and it is to each one of us that the Lord's Word is directed.

If we would seek the origin of these readings, we would have to delve into the most ancient of Christian usages, and to go, in fact, even beyond them to practices dear to the heart of devout Israel. The Service of the synagogue knew such readings from the Law and the Prophets.[1] Have we not seen Jesus reading Isaias to his fellow Jews (Luke 4:16, 21), and did not St. Paul, while on his missionary journeys, take part in similar readings? (Cf. Acts 13:14, 16). The early church faithfully preserved this usage: reading from the sacred books bulked large in the primitive liturgies, and it would be surprising to the first Christians were they now to return and hear only the two brief scraps which are left in to-day's Mass, in its Epistle and Gospel.

In older times, first readings from the Old Testament, then some of the Apostolic Letters, and finally a section of the Gospel itself, were read out for the people to hear and think about. It is this three-part division of preparatory readings which even yet lingers on in the venerable service of Good Friday.[2] At first, these readings were neither brief nor formally delimited beforehand, as they were later made; and the reader used to go on uninterruptedly until the bishop saw fit to signal him that he thought enough had been proposed for the instruction of his hearers. It was only with the appearance of the Roman Missal of 1570 that there came into general usage the two previously selected fragments or pericopes, accommodated to the feast being celebrated.

The first passage which is ordinarily read is the *Epistle.* As this name—*epistola*—indicates, it is a passage from a letter. On Sundays this apostolic letter is almost always taken from the writings of the Apostle Paul. On other occasions—on saints' days, on Lenten ferias, and on Ember days—it is generally from the prophetic writings of the Old Testament that instruction is proposed to us in the reading, which is then termed *Lectio* or Lesson from . . . (whatever its source may happen to be). Evidently, in either case the liturgical purpose is the same, for it shows that in the beginning God speaks to us by the agency of intermediaries, by the mouth of men who are His witnesses or confessors, who are inspired by Him to prepare us that we may later receive His own message directly; and for this reason the reading is done in the name of the Lord.[3]

66

As AT THE WATERS of Babylon the exiles of Israel were spurred to hope by the voice of Your prophets,

as oppressed Israel found in reading and re-reading the books of Your Law the most certain guardian of their fidelity to You,

as, in its beginnings, Your Church learned, from the reading of the Apostolic Letters, of the joy and the love brought us by Our Saviour,

and as, in days of severe trial Your martyrs found in those apostolic words the motive of their self-sacrifice;

grant, my Lord, that these words of Your chosen witnesses may find my soul tilled, fertile, and ready to bear in joy the fruit of faith;

grant that I may be prepared for that Word by which You have spoken to men from the foundation of the world:

for it is of the Voice of Your Word, my Lord, that it is written that it brings loneliness to an end and fills the heart with strength;

it was that Voice which, on one harvest day, cast Your enemy Saul to the ground and, with a single word, won his heart.

VIII

An Interval of Preparation

BETWEEN THE EPISTLE AND THE GOSPEL

Between the *Epistle* and the *Gospel* we find a group of prayers and chants which might readily be taken by the hasty observer to be mere digressions; no more, that is to say, than bypaths leading away from the general plan of the liturgy; but they are actually most meaningful.

The reading is brought to a close by the usual formulary expressive of thanks—*Deo gratias,* "thanks be to God"—words found so often in the Pauline Epistles, and expressing the notion that we offer thanks because God willed the words that we have just heard to be said or written.

It was the custom in the old Israelitish liturgy that the course of the reading or didactic service be broken by the recitation of psalms. This at once avoided the tedium of monotony and made certain a real participation of the congregation in worship. The chants which are found in our Missal for the present interval are a survival of this usage. That it is a very old usage among the Christians themselves is evident from the testimony of Tertullian in the third century. There are three of these chanted formularies. The *Gradual* is ordinarily composed of words which appropriately refer back to the lesson just read; and it was anciently begun by a singer standing on the step (*gradus*) of the lectern. To his versicle, the congregation

replied by taking up a refrain. The *Alleluia* is an old Judaic expression of joy, and is of immemorial usage: it recalls the Lord's coming, and so serves to introduce the *Gospel*. The *Tract* takes the place of the *Alleluia* on days of penance or in seasons of sorrow. It was designed for the voices of the great solo singers of the past, to be sung uninterruptedly by them without the intervention of the choir; and being set to solemn and noble music it is redolent of antiquity. To these formularies the liturgists of the Middle Ages added the *Sequence* or *Prose*, a sort of poetic commentary on the feast being celebrated.

The words of the sequence were originally set to that long series of melismatic neumes in which the *Alleluia* seems to prolong itself in bursts of great and continued joy. These *Proses* are most admirable expressions of Christian fervor: our present Missal retains the *Victimae paschali* for Easter Day, the *Lauda Sion* for Corpus Christi, the *Veni sancte Spiritus* for Whitsunday, the *Dies irae* for Requiem Masses, and that most touching of all, the *Stabat Mater,* which Jacapone da Todi wrote in praise of Our Lady in her Compassion.

There is no doubt that these are but adjuncts to the primitive liturgy; but who can be blind to the splendor they lend it?

70

Now the book is brought to its privileged place, to the left side of the altar as we face it, to the side, as it were, of the heart, wherefrom the words of Christ Himself are to resound. Meanwhile, the priest who is about to speak in Christ's name, prepares himself for that awesome task by begging that God will purify his lips as once did He those of Isaias when an angel touched the great prophet's mouth with a burning coal.

Munda cor. Cleanse my heart; for Your burning coal has more to do than just to make pure these my faithless lips, hitherto so ready to mouth words of anger or of folly;

there are also my ears to be made pure, for they have been over-willing to choose the jangling discords of the world above Your Word; they have welcomed the Lie more easily than the Truth;

there are my eyes, so slow to open to the light because of their fondness for the things of darkness;

there is indeed all my being which waits in need of the purifying fire of Your angel; there is my soul, my judgment, my imagination, and my sinful heart which has betrayed You.

Munda cor. Cleanse my heart; may all my taints and stains be burnt away, and with them all that I know to be foul in me, all that is darksome and hateful to You.

Grant that Your Word may stir in me unfailing faithfulness, rousing me to the love that turns not back but ever moves forward into Your marvelous glad Light.

IX

The Word of God

THE GOSPEL

We are now come to the climax of the Ante-Mass. Up to this point, we have heard the divine message from the lips of men: it is now God Himself who speaks to us! Christ comes to teach us by the example of His life and by His own words.[1]

And it is for this reason that from the very early days of the primitive church, this reading of the *Gospel* has been considered an essential element in the liturgy: in the catacombs it was already something that no one ever thought of dispensing with. This high point in the preparation for the Sacrifice emphasizes the fact that the Christ who came to undergo death for the salvation of each and every one of us is the self-same who teaches each and every one of us what to believe and what to do.

Therefore it is that this point in the Mass is marked and surrounded by an especial degree of solemnity. Is not the Gospel Book another symbol of the Master? Is it not the book which St. John Chrysostom said he could never open without a feeling of awe? At chanted Masses, incense and lights, and at low Masses, the significant gestures of the priest in placing his hand upon the book and in kissing it and marking it with the Cross, express the spirit of veneration due this book.

Having signed themselves with the Cross upon their foreheads, their lips, and their breasts, the congregation listen to the reading of the Gospel while they stand respectfully attentive. The signing of themselves triply with the Cross is to indicate their intellectual acceptance of Truth, their readiness to confess it, and their heartfelt attachment to it.

Ever since the sixth century there has become more and more widespread the present custom of selecting in advance a pericope from one or another of the Four Gospels; and the determining idea in this selection has been to offer an embodiment of the particular lesson which the day's Mass is to reveal to us.

All the other parts of the proper Mass formularies are in dependence, more or less marked, to the Gospel pericope: they serve either as commentaries in respect to what has been declared by it, or as assurances in respect to the fulfillment of that declaration.

This, then, is a point of culmination. It is the very voice of the Incarnate God Himself to which we now listen. And when the reading of His Word is brought to an end, and the voice of our own faith has been raised to acclaim Christ our Master and our Teacher, the whole purpose of the sermon which follows lies, in principle at least, in nothing other than an attempt to develop, to explain, to comment upon the Master's words, that in those words our minds may find enlightenment and our hearts enrichment.

CHRIST SPEAKS TO YOU: hear Him! In these words are the tidings of His life and of His teachings; and they are one.

He is the Child conceived of the Holy Ghost in a Virgin's womb,

He is the new-born Babe in the manger, destined for lowliness and obscurity,

He is the son of a workman, and is Himself a workman, one who knew how to handle the carpenter's tools;

it is He who spoke from the Galilean hills and by the shores of the Lake of Tiberius,

it is He who healed the Centurion's servant, who becalmed the tempest and called Lazarus back to mortal life;

He it is who is man's exemplar, the model of perfection, the pattern none can surpass:

all this is here; listen as He speaks!

It is He who teaches men to love one another,

to pardon enemies and to receive them as brethren,

to be pure as He was, and to be meek and lowly of heart, as well;

it is He who teaches men to live always in their heavenly Father's sight, as He himself did;

He it is who alone fully embodies love, truth, justice, the supreme realities which mean more than earthly life:

listen; listen as He speaks!

And inasmuch as He was affronted by hatred, by betrayal, by abandonment into the hands of wicked men,

inasmuch as in His human flesh He suffered more than you can ever suffer,

since He died as you shall die, but more horribly, being given over to the dread infamy of a felon's end;

therefore did He give you an example to follow, by revealing that Death is swallowed up in Victory,

for you, being ransomed by Him, are destined and promised to Life Eternal:

therefore, my heart, listen as He speaks.

X

The Homily

THE WORD OF GOD EXPLAINED

Preaching, as a part of our service of worship, is as old as the coming among men of Our Incarnate Lord. In fact, unless we speak of the grace of the actual presence of Jesus among His contemporaries, it is prior to the introduction of the Christian sacramental system itself. It was the method chosen by Our Lord to announce His Gospel. And before Our Lord's preaching John the Baptist had proclaimed, in the voice of one crying in the wilderness, that He whom the prophets had foretold was come. An explanation of the sacred writings had long been a feature in the synagogue service; and was not Our Lord following this tradition when, at the age of twelve, He was found by His Mother in the Temple, disputing with the Doctors of the Law?

Fides est ex auditu; "Faith comes by hearing"; and St. Paul, himself a great preacher, gives us the reason for this by asking how hearing shall be without a preacher; and how shall there be a preacher unless one be sent?[1] These two ideas, touching the office of preacher and the fact of his mission, have always been held in honor in the Christian *ecclesia.* Many Breviary readings, which explain the Gospels appointed at various Masses of the liturgical cycle, are taken from sermons actually preached in past years: among the Latins, St. Augustine, St. Leo, St. Ambrose, St. Gregory the Great, St. Hilary, St. Bernard; among the Greeks, St. John Chrysostom, St. Gregory Nazianzene, St. John of Damascus—are their authors. They

have their successors today, as they have had in every period; *for faith comes by hearing;* and the continuation of preaching is vital to the maintenance of the Faith. At first, the bishops alone were the preachers or spokesmen for the Church; but, in time, these successors of the Apostles themselves began to depute others to aid them. In the very dawn of the Church, St. Paul sends Timothy to be the overseer of a church which he himself had founded; and he reminds its members that he *had kept back nothing that was profitable to them:* that he had *taught them publicly and from house to house:* that by *the space of three years he had ceased not to warn everyone night and day with tears.*[2] Historically, the deacons, originally dispensers of the Church's charity, were particularly identified with preaching. Nowadays the office of preaching is a chief duty of the priesthood; and rectors of parishes, who share with bishops the task of being shepherds of the flock of Christ, are invested by the Church with the exercise of this function which they may delegate to their assistant priests.

Our Lord's sermons were usually preached to the multitude and are marvelous examples of directness: He tells his hearers a story; and, instead of dealing with abstractions, He personifies its moral elements. However, when He speaks within the circle of His chosen twelve, as in His discourse at the Last Supper, we see Him making use of ideas and of a manner of speech more abstract in na-

ture and development. And this pattern was followed by St. Paul, who, addressing a sophisticated audience in Athens, tempered his manner to their habits of thought, quoting the pagan writers then held in esteem.

The Church has always placed emphasis upon preaching as a part of its worship and praise, a service directed in one sense to God, and in another to human hearers; and conciliar decrees and canons join in exhorting the clergy to be careful in their performance of this duty. The Council of Trent, to which much is owed for the preservation of the Catholic Faith in the modern world, embodied the practice of the Church in its re-quirement that on Sundays and festivals the Gospel selection read during the liturgy be explained to the congregation. Both the Code of Canon Law and the liturgical books re-echo this prescription. The Second Council of the Vatican has again voiced the Church's traditional teaching by recalling the privileged place of the homily in our corporate worship; and it stipulates that, at Masses of precept, when the people are present, an explanation be given of some passage at least from the liturgical office being celebrated, preference being given to the assigned readings from the Scriptures.

I N THE READING FROM THE GOSPEL, which I have just listened to at this Mass, it is Your own Voice that I have heard, my Lord: now there comes to me the voice of the interpreter of that life-giving Word. Grant, O Master and Teacher, that I may profit from what I am about to hear. Unstop my ears, fatigued by the myriad voices of this world, that they may be open to Your message. Enlighten my mind, bemused by the clamor of false prophets, that it may be receptive to the lesson I should now learn. Inflame my heart, betrayed by wayward inclination, that I may be willing to do what You command.

I offer, too, O Lord, my own poor prayers for those who preach Your Word; arm them with the sharp sword of Your Spirit; endue them with Your own divine persuasiveness; grant that they may bring us Your message in such terms as will quicken the understanding of all their hearers. May the tongues of preachers not show forth only the words of human wisdom; may they proclaim the Truth uniquely revealed by You, my Master, the Way, the Truth, and the Life.

XI

The Canon of our Faith

THE CREDO

All that He has come to teach me, that do I believe with all the strength of my soul! Such is the intent and purpose of the Creed.

From the earliest days of Christianity, the emission of an act of faith was a pre-requisite for being baptized. No doubt, the formulary was then very simple, something perhaps in the nature of the declaration made by the Ethiopian officer to Philip the Deacon, when he said: "I believe that Jesus Christ is the Son of God" (Acts 8:37). But it was not long before error launched itself at the principles of Christian faith, and from this there arose the necessity of stating those principles in precise and definite terms.

It was to satisfy this need that there were drawn up *Symbols,* brief affirmations, concrete propositions of belief—"the canons of our faith," as they were called in third century Africa.

The old *Apostles' Creed,* whose direct and definite statements are familiar to our private prayers, did not suit the exigencies aroused when the great heresies of the fourth century opened questions inevitably attendant upon any attempt to discern the nature of Christ in relation to the persons of the divine Trinity. So it was that, at two Councils—one held in Nicea in 325, the other at Constantinople in 381—there was drawn up the text of a more elaborate symbol or state-ment of belief. It is this Creed that we find in our Sunday Masses.

First at Antioch, and then later at Constantinople, it was decided to insert the Creed in the Mass formulary. The usage spread to Spain, to France, and into the Germanies; but Rome itself did not adopt it until after the year 1000.[1]

In our own time, the use of the *Credo* is limited to Masses said on Sundays (even though the Office of the Sunday yield to some high-ranking feast, not otherwise entitled to the Creed, or to some privileged votive Mass), on certain major feasts, during the octaves of Christmas, Easter, and Pentecost, and on the occasion of certain other Masses which particularly concern the whole Christian community.[2] The celebrant intones the Creed with profound fervor and then the faithful of the congregation, standing, proclaim it aloud and unanimously. "Let the Creed resound," ordered a Council held at Toledo in Spain in 589, "so that the true faith may be declared in song, and that the souls of believers, in accepting that faith, may be made ready to partake, in communion, of the Body and Blood of Christ."

In the Gospel the Word has spoken to men; now Incarnate, He will come to offer Himself upon the altar. The *Credo* thus becomes a link between two parts of the Mass.

82

I WOULD that each time I join in the *Credo,*
There might re-echo the joy of my baptismal song,
Voicing aloud the strength of my faith
And my heart's cleaving to my Lord!

I would that the whys and the wherefores of my faith,
I, standing with my brethren, might proudly proclaim,
Just as once it was, and may again be
In the face of terror unleashed on the fold.

I would that my deep loyalty I might now declare
To my holy Mother, the Church, dear keeper of my faith;
For the words she has taught, she has herself learned
'Neath the unfailing shade of the radiant Spirit's wing!

XII

The Offertory

PRAYERS AT THE OFFERING

The Ante-Mass, or Liturgy of the Word, which has now come to its conclusion, was historically known as "the Mass of the Catechumens," because those who were but aspirants to the faith were anciently bidden to depart from the assembly after the proclamation of the act of faith. As well as the nonbaptized, sinners who were making public profession of penitence were dismissed; none but full members of the Christian band who were themselves, so to speak, "in good standing," were permitted to attend the holy mysteries which now open in the fuller sense. Within the closed company of the faithful, there was upraised a series of prayers to voice the collective intention of the Church standing on the verge of the holy of holies. Of these prayers Trent's Missal preserved only some short and tantalizing reminders: the versicle *Dominus vobiscum* with its customary response, and the injunction *Oremus*. But recently, provision has been made for the restoration of these ancient prayers in places where the bishop judges it to be desirable.[1]

The first sacramental act of the Mass takes place at the Offertory, which is now marked by a group of six prayers. Of these one differs from day to day, being specifically adapted to the day or festival being observed;[2] the other five are fixed, having as their aim the presentation to God not alone of the offerings but of those who make those offerings as well. How full of meaning was the old ceremonial which marked this moment in the early church! The congregation indicated unmistakably their share in the act of offering by going themselves, in procession, to present their gifts. What were these gifts? Bread and wine, first of all; but also other edible substances, and even other things, such as gold and silver, even birds and flowers. The deacons sorted out these gifts on a special table, and they placed on one side all that would be used in the sacrifice; on the other they piled up what would be given to the poor. A responsive or antiphonal chant was sung during this procession, and it would appear that the Offertory must have been among the most striking parts of the Mass.

By the time of the Middle Ages this usage had gradually been done away with, no doubt because of the germ of possible disorder which lay within it. Our time has seen an effort at a symbolic revival of this open participation; and in some places the beautiful suggestion is made to the people that they themselves put into the ciborium the particles which are to be consecrated.[3] There are also many other current usages which recall the primitive offertory: the collection of money has in view the same charitable end, while the community aspect is evoked whenever the custom is established of families taking turn in supplying the bread to be used. The same may be said, as well, of the offering or stipend which is given to the priest whom we request to say a special Mass for us; for in such a case the gift and the

intention may be regarded as being linked. But, of course, the very essence of all these usages is comprehended in the prayerful words which the priest now says in our name. When he holds, with both his hands, the paten on which he has placed the host, and when he lifts it up in a gesture of magnificent supplication, it is in truth as the representative of all of us that he now sets forth and presents our oblation to the Lord.

I WISH that this bread and this wine which the priest now offers to You, my Lord, may be in Your sight as truly bread of mine, as truly wine of mine. For just as if I were living in those earlier days when I might myself have brought them to the table set near Your altar, it is I myself who now unite in offering bread and wine to You.

It is my will to be truly a participant in Your Mass, in Your Sacrifice, in firmness of faith and in depth of feeling, in attentive devotion, and in worthy reception of this sacrament;

for I wish to join myself to this unbroken offering which, throughout the centuries, Your Church has daily held aloft before Your face.

It is my wish to be one among my fellows, to be a sharer in the society that finds its link of union in You, to be one of Your own flock, so that in seeking my own salvation I may also be of avail in effecting the salvation of all mankind.

Now, therefore, to You, my Lord, do I entrust myself, into Your hands do I give myself, so that all I pray for may come to be; so that my offering may find favor in Your sight.

XIII

By Bread and Wine

THE PREPARATION OF THE BREAD AND WINE

At the Offertory there begins that setting-apart of the material substances to be offered to God, a setting-apart which will reach its culmination at the *Consecration*. It is prescribed that two kinds of material substances be thus marked for presentation to God: these are bread and wine. Such were the elements chosen by Jesus Himself at the Last Supper to be the perceptible signs of the self-immolation he there made. How fitting it is that these humble and quite ordinary fruits of the earth should be made the instrumentalities whereby the Saviour comes to mankind: bread is that staff of life of which we never outgrow the need, while in the drinking of wine our thirst is rather whetted than sated. Was it not that he might be cheered and strengthened by it that wine was given to Noah after the terrors of the Deluge?

In the beginning, the bread offered at Mass was the ordinary bread of daily use, but it was of the best kind available, marked by the Cross after having been made in the shape of rounded flat biscuits that it might the more easily be broken. From about the ninth century *azyme* bread began to be used, recalling that non-fermented, unleavened bread which Jesus, in observing the Law of Moses, would have used, and did use, at the Last Supper. The Mass wine is simply the juice of "the fruit of the vine," which in His own life-time on earth the Master was ac-

customed to drink. By a custom which dates only from the fourteenth century white wine is often used now for evident reasons of cleanliness, although these reasons are somewhat neglectful of the more striking symbol of blood which the use of red wine would afford.

In the long view of the whole matter, the bread and the wine become, from the moment they are first offered to God, symbols of Christ's body and blood; and it is as such that they are now viewed by the soul; for the Offertory anticipates, as it were, the *Consecration*. A liturgical act emphasizes this: the priest adds a little water to the wine in the chalice, so that the two liquids may blend, just as in Christ the nature of the Word and the nature of His Sacred Humanity are inseparable, just as the Master and His Church are one. During the Middle Ages it was widely believed, as well, that by this water was also figured that which came from the pierced side of the crucified Jesus; [1] and, in a touching rite, the Greek liturgy prescribes the use of a small lancet in the Mass, whereby the host is transfixed in memory of that wounded side.

"We offer unto you, O Lord, this chalice of salvation," now says the priest, signifying that in mystic manner the bread will become flesh and the wine in the chalice blood: the Sacrament is already coming into being.

IF YOU HAVE naught else to lay before the Lord, deliver unto Him at least your labors and your pain;

many are the men who have striven mightily that this fragment of bread might rest here upon the paten.

If your hands are empty and your voice stricken dumb, offer at least your wounded heart and all that it has borne;

that this chalice might hold this wine, was it not needful that the grape be crushed and yield its all?

If you have nothing but sin and bitterness, a life that is tedious and full of sharp distress,

at least hold before heaven your hands so pitiably laden, manifesting to the divine mercy your need to be received at His table.

If you lack the mere strength to pray and entreat, if there is naught in your heart but emptiness and disorder,

then silently yield into the hands of Another all your being, and you shall find in Him both Gift and Giver.

XIV

With Clean Hands

THE WASHING OF THE CELEBRANT'S HANDS

Following the Offertory at solemn Masses the priest incenses the altar, just as he had done at the beginning of the Mass of the Catechumens. This recalls the "fragrant sacrifices" beloved of Israel; and it is a ceremonial act of deep meaning. The perfume of the incense ascends to God as does a prayer. "There was another angel that came and took his stand at the altar, with a censer of gold," says the writer of the *Apocalypse,* "and incense was given him in plenty, so that he could make an offering on the golden altar before the throne, out of the prayers said by all the saints." (8:3–4).

In the event, it has now become customary at *all* Masses to carry out at this point a liturgical act which in its origin was primarily a response to a practical necessity: by the washing of his hands, which had touched the general offerings of the congregation as well as the incense-bearing thurible, the celebrant cleansed them in anticipation of taking up the bread about to become the body of Christ. It was usual, aforetime, that this washing be performed at the Epistle side of the altar where there used to stand a basin hewn from the rock of the church wall. Does not this act even now serve to maintain the old tradition of the Judaic lustral purification? It may also be regarded as having the same sense as that old-time washing in a fountain before the church door, a washing of which the people now keep the meaning by dipping their fingers in the holy water basin as they come in. But here again the symbolic sense offers its own justification, so that, as in baptism, water which cleanses the body is thought of as purifying the soul. This thought is enforced by the verse of the twenty-fifth Psalm which the priest now recites: "*Lavabo inter innocentes manus meas...*" I will wash my hands in innocency, my Lord, and then I will do my sacred duty at your altar.

94

WITHIN MY BEING there is so deep-seated a stain that not all the fountains of this world can wash it out.

That stain clings so firmly to every fibre of my being as entirely to impregnate it, having become, indeed, part of myself.

There is no one of my thoughts or actions but sharply recalls to me

that I am tainted within and without; that, despite all my distaste for evil, what I would not, that I yet do.

Is there, then, to be found any water, any water unlike the waters of this earth,

is there a stream wholly pure, chastely untainted, and everlastingly clean?

Can there be any laver so marvellously fit as to wash from my being this innermost crassness,

a laver that will cleanse the dregs of hidden shame from the darksome fen that is my soul?

All this Your grace can do, my Lord . . .

Now, therefore, let it stream upon my head, running down upon my shoulders and covering me;

may it re-effect all that was done in the baptismal font from which I rose new-born to You;

may it run down and search out all those darksome corners, hidden, unavowed, and scarce acknowledged even to myself;

may it restore to me a purity all unspotted, such a purity as marks regained childhood's clear-eyed joy.

XV

To the Three Divine Persons

PRAYER TO THE HOLY TRINITY

When he has come back to the center of the altar the priest bows in silence. The part which he is to take in the sacrifice, properly so called, now lies immediately before him; he therefore withdraws for an instant into appropriate recollection. The prayer which he then says seems to have the form of some prayer of private devotion; and it was, as a matter of fact, unknown to the primitive Roman liturgy. Nevertheless, it is quite ancient, being commonly ascribed to St. Ambrose, the great bishop of fourth-century Milan. Its official appearance in the Mass dates from about the twelfth century; but even today the Carthusians do not make use of it in their liturgy.[1]

Suscipe, Sancta Trinitas, hanc oblationem "Receive, O Holy Trinity, this oblation . . ." We may note that almost all the prayers of the Mass are addressed to the Father or to the Son, to the Father through the Son; but here direct address is made to the Trinity. This demonstrates the importance of this prayer: it offers an opportunity to take stock, as it were, of the deep meaning of the sacrifice which is about to be offered in high religious avowal of the fullness of God's divinity seated in the Blessed Trinity. Moreover, the text itself is full of suggestive significance: first it refers to several of the capital events in the life of Our Lord—His Passion, Resurrection, and Ascension. (More logically, the old rite of Lyon here begins by recalling the Incarnation and the Nativity.)[2] Then this prayer goes on to make mention of those great saints who stand before the Throne of the august Trinity as special intercessors for mankind. Thus does it recall to our minds the two determining reasons we have for the hope of glory which is in us.

TO BE SAVED—I do not know precisely all that this means, my Lord. What is Salvation but the fact of coming to a knowledge of all that You are? And is not this something which is beyond discerning by the fleshly eyes of mortals? Yet this much I do know—for shattering experience has so taught me—I can never be saved of myself alone.

Of You, one God in three Persons, Holy Writ tells us that no man can see Your Face and not die. In Your sight I search myself, and I find and acknowledge that I am nothing: I am but a fleeting and miserable object before the everlasting and all-powerful Fashioner of mankind; my flesh is laden with sin, my soul is tainted and stained as I kneel before the Great Exemplar, the one Model of perfection. I confess that my judgment is varying and uncertain, my comprehension but weak and vain, being indeed, no more than a feeble rush-light which vanishes in the all-consuming brilliance of that Spirit who knows and tries all that is.

Nevertheless, I know that my God took upon Himself flesh like unto my own: He lived, He suffered, and He died just as I do and shall. Yet He is not wholly like me, for did He not rise again after death, did He not rise of His own power? It is because He did so rise, and because I know it with entire certainty, that the hope of salvation swells up in my soul. It is through the Son, God in man made manifest, that I shall, one day, know the Father in the dazzling clarity of the Spirit.

And I have a cloud of witnesses—all those who have passed beyond and have gained God's presence. My hope rests upon experience and is buoyed up by it; for there once walked on earth a woman called Mary, men called John the Baptist, Peter, and Paul, and countless others. They now stand close to that Presence before whom nothing defiled may come; they stand interceding for me, inspiring me. Inasmuch as all these have known Your Grace, my Lord, why may not I?

XVI

The Oblation

THE PRAYER OVER THE OBLATIONS

The third portion of the Mass is over: I have *prayed;* I have *listened;* I have *made my offering.* The priest now kisses the altar and urgently begs the congregation to unite themselves with him in order to take part in his offering, and here it is that he seems to pause in what he is doing that he may make a final and most pressing appeal to them before he proceeds to the Consecration. He does this in the words of a medieval prayer, the *Orate fratres,* which is a sort of long-drawn-out *Oremus.* It expresses in marvelous fashion the full sense of this, his final injunction to the bystanders to join with heartfelt sincerity in what he is about to do: "This sacrificial act of mine is yours as well." It is as though he said: "Be mindful that I do not make this offering alone, but together with you!" [1]

And it is as if in answer to this appeal that we have at this point in the Mass the second of the three great imprecatory invocations, the Prayers over the Gifts or Oblations, the others being the *Collects* and the *Postcommunions.* Of great antiquity, harking back to the same age as the Collect, which it resembles also in style, the Prayer over the Oblations is, like it, addressed to the Triune God in Unity, on behalf of the whole body of Christians. The Prayer over the Oblations was formerly called the *Secreta.* Many explanations were offered for this: one suggested that in contrast to the Collect—the prayer of the *plebs collecta* [2]—this was a prayer proper to the chosen ones, to the

faithful, as distinct from the greater assembly which had, until an earlier point in the Mass, included the catechumens as well. Another suggested that it should rather be taken as having reference to the oblations of bread and wine which are now set apart, or secreted,[3] from the other offerings. Still another took the name to indicate that what we have here is a prayer of introduction to the *secret things,* to the King's mysteries. Whatever be the historical origin of the term, the *Ordo Missae* of 1965 now terms it *Oratio super oblata* and directs that it be chanted in all sung Masses and be recited aloud in all other Masses. It thus takes its place, openly, alongside the two other prayers, proper to each Mass, of which it forms a sort of central pendant. The straightforward and telling phrases of this prayer vary according to the Mass Proper which is being used, and they express the characteristic spirit of the day being celebrated. In accordance with that ascensional, or upward-striving, note which marks the progress of the liturgical action from the beginning of the Offertory, these prayers give evidence, when they are contrasted with the Collects, of an increase in fervor and assurance. They all display one grand, dominating idea: I know that these fruits of the earth, which are my gift to God, will be returned to me after they have been touched by the fecund blessing of His inexhaustibly bounteous hand. I know that they are my pledge or earnest of heaven, and of that everlasting life which He will give me.

ARNESTLY DO I VOICE this prayer as it bespeaks the feelings of my innermost heart: it is a song of hope and of comfort as I struggle with dark and oppressive fears.

My Lord, well do I know that my gift to You is less than nothing, being but a morsel of bread and a few drops of wine poured into Your Cup, while nothing could be less worthy of being accepted by You than my own miserable self.

But will you dwell upon the worth of what is offered to You? When weighed in the balance with You what is there but will be found wanting? It is only the upward thrust of joyous confidence holding out these trifling gifts to You, it is only the plea of faith that begs You to accept them, that finds favor in Your sight.

I know that in return for a single grain of wheat You can grant a most abundant harvest; for one word spoken in mercy, the fullness of Your all-embracing pardon; for a simple draught of cold water given in Your Name, that Living Water which quenches undying thirst; and that to him who takes up and bears Your Cross, You will grant Gilead's balm.

Therefore, my Lord, as, in singleness of heart and full generously, I offer You all that I have been, all that I am, and all that I shall become, I know that Your boundless Love will enrich me a thousandfold with peace, with true happiness, and with hope.

XVII

The Prologue to the Great Thanksgiving

THE PREFACE

We are approaching the climax of our worship as we begin that great prayer which now initiates the sacrificial part of the Mass, the true re-enactment of the sacrifice of the Cross. We are come to the *Canon*, that is to say as this Greek word tells us, to the part of the ceremony which is the *rule* and measure of it all, determining its lines and its whole meaning. Of great antiquity, and stemming, indeed, directly from that Last Supper which it reproduces, this *action*—to use the term which the early Christians employed—gives us pause both by reason of its architectonic magnificence and because of the stately simplicity of its formularies. The Canon can be divided into seven sections, of which the Consecration is the focal point.

Now the priest cries out to all the people: *Sursum corda*—"Lift up your hearts"; this is the moment when your thoughts should be set on God alone. The celebrant stands with uplifted hands as though he would bear aloft the compelling expectation of the congregation. With one voice the people acclaim the Lord on whom their hearts are fixed. This is just what was anciently done in the old Church of Africa in the days of that great and holy bishop, Cyprian of Carthage.

The Gospel tells us that before He blessed the wine of the Supper, Christ our Lord gave thanks to God; and this is, indeed, so essential a part of our worship that the word *Eucharist* which describes it has come to be used of the whole Sacrifice itself. Therefore is it that with *the giving of thanks* is begun the action which is the very heart of the Mass. First of all, the celebrant says—or rather he declaims—the *Preface*. How aptly does this word (which has been in use since the third century) convey the purpose of this prayer. The Preface is the introduction to the sacrifice, the eucharistic prologue, the thanksgiving which, according to the institution of Christ, must precede the Consecration.[1] It is, moreover, a reminder to us of those elaborate and abundant extemporaneous prayers which, in primitive times, faith and love brought to birth on the lips of the officiant.[2] In modern times, there has been a tendency to think of the Preface as being separate from the Canon; but it may truly be felt that to that Canon is intimately linked this prayer so pure in its style that it seems to have been born in the depths of the human heart and thence to thrust itself upward toward the Summit which is God. The Greek and Armenian churches have but one Preface to be used throughout the entire year, while at Rome there used to be a different one for each day.[3] This principle of the variable Preface is now maintained in the sixteen which our modern Missal retains, in

accommodation to the varying seasons and feasts of the liturgical year. All of them are constructed in similar form and style and show that they are rooted in the same motivation. They stress that the Sacrifice is offered to God, the Lord Almighty, and that this is done by, and in the Name of Jesus Christ. Each of the Prefaces, in its turn, recalls what it is that has been done by Him to effect our salvation. For the very reason that the Preface thus touches in its intention upon what is by nature ineffable, it is fitting that the angels of the heavenly court be called upon to join with us in it, and they are accordingly invoked to the greater glory of God.

CAN YOU NOW impel yourself, my heart, above your own concerns, and rise to the things of God?

Consider what hours you allot, each day, to the perishing wrecks of time, and how brief is your vigil for everlasting life.

The moment has come to be still: it is now that, in fullness of heart and with confidence unbounded,

you must draw apart and impel yourself upward!

For this much you know: these mystic rites are your own; they are the very life of your life.

This you know: there can be no greater, no truer joy for you than the joy born of this divine confrontation.

This you know: the Son of God, in taking flesh from the womb of the Virgin; Mary, in freely becoming the Mother of Sorrows; the Man-God, in deigning to live your life, to share with you the pangs of mortal death, to come, even as you shall, to the tomb;

all this they did, as you know, only for you.

All this indeed you know. Yet it is only in the long-awaited fulfillment of heavenly union that the rich floods of this knowing shall water the dry ground of your selfhood's uttermost limits.

XVIII

Sanctus, Sanctus, Sanctus

THE THREE-FOLD ACCLAMATION

TO THE ALL-HOLY

It is in united acknowledgment of the stupendous glory of God that celebrant, ministers, choir, and congregation raise their voices in the chant of the *Sanctus*, the culmination of the Preface, and the fuller revelation of its meaning. Its thrice-repeated acclamation contrasts strongly with the flowing periods of the introductory prayer just chanted or declaimed by the priest; it seems to perpetuate the ecstatic tones of that seraphic hymn which fell upon the entranced ear of the prophet Isaias as he responded to the divine call that he enter upon the mission entrusted to him. Set at this point in the Mass, it serves to remind us that it is God Who, in His holiness, can alone bring brightness to the night of our mortal days.[1]

Not every one of the ancient liturgies knew this hymn, although its institution is attributed to St. Sixtus I, who, as Pope, introduced it into the Mass in the second century. Today, it is part of all liturgies, being called the *Sanctus* among the Latins and the *Trisagion* among the Greeks.[2]

It falls into two parts. The first of these brings to mind a mysterious passage in Isaias, wherein that prophet tells us of his vision of God (6: 1–3): "I saw the Lord sitting upon a throne that towered high above me, the skirts of his robe filling the Temple. Above it rose the figures of the seraphim, each of them six-winged; with two wings they veiled God's face, with two his feet, and the other two kept them poised in flight. And ever the same words passed between them, Holy, holy, holy is the Lord God of hosts; all the earth is full of His glory!" It is in recollection of our heritage from that old Israel of promise that we Christians still make liturgical use of the Hebrew word *Sabaoth*,[3] as we sing to the Lord of hosts.

The second part of the hymn takes up the same theme, and calls upon the Powers of Heaven to help us in glorifying the One Lord. Does not the *Hosanna in excelsis* recall the song of the angels at Bethlehem on Christmas night? And here is a reference to Christ; for this *hosanna* (another Hebrew word) is followed by the very formulary which men used to salute the Messiah at His solemn entry into the holy City: "Blessed is He who comes in the name of the Lord."[4]

110

Now is God-in-man-made-manifest truly about to come among us. As the words of this hymn are said, He enters into the core of this sacramental action just as, aforetime, He came into Jerusalem, there to ascend His throne, the throne of the Cross.

WHEN I PONDER within my heart, my Lord, on Your Glory and on the limitless power that lies within Your hand;

when I consider the vastness of Your creation, and peer into endless vistas of space; when I recollect that behind all that is, behind all that has been, You are;

when I reflect that for uncounted aeons of years, Your Spirit has hovered unsearchably over the destiny of men;

then do I ask, how—even were all the angelic choirs to lend me their voices that I might more worthily hymn Your unexampled holiness—

then do I ask, as I bend in love while my mind reels before the unfathomed mystery of Your nature,

then do I ask how it can be that You, centering in Yourself the Perfection of all Glory, nevertheless regard my nothingness;

how it is that You are mindful of me and reveal to me the secret of Yourself and all Your being as You suffer a drop of Your divine blood to fall on the face of a sinner?

XIX

The Church at the Foot of the Cross

THE REMEMBRANCE OF THE LIVING

Te igitur . . .—"Wherefore, O most merciful Father, we humbly beseech You, through Your Son, Jesus Christ, our Lord, that you would be pleased to receive these gifts, these presented offerings . . ." It is in these words that the brilliant interruption made by the *Sanctus* in the unfolding of the ideas first expressed in the *Preface* is bridged over (as the word *igitur*[1] indicates), in order that there may be resumed the series of prayers leading directly to the *Consecration.* Here, indeed, begins the Canon strictly so-called, and it was this consideration which moved the miniaturists of the Middle Ages to paint the initial letter T of *Te igitur* in such wondrous style. How well does this letter figure the Cross; and it is, in fact, the origin of those Crucifixion scenes which are found in most Missals at this point in the text.

The hour of the Sacrifice has come; the celebrant now moves more solemnly than hitherto, all his motions are charged with a consciousness of their mystic meaning as he progresses from action to action, now joining his hands, now raising his eyes to heaven, again kissing the altar once more; and then, having made the three-fold sign of the Cross over the *oblata,* he finally extends his hands, palms downward, over the chalice and the host, in the manner of one who gives testimony under oath.

There are five prayers said in a low voice before the Consecration of the Elements. Their sequence is not wholly smooth, nor is it devoid of awkwardness and interruption; for they are the result of a series of dislocations and developments covering several centuries. For example, the first of them (*Te igitur*) and the last (*Quam oblationem*) belong, most certainly, to the Canon in its very oldest form; the list of saints who are called to memory (in the *Communicantes*) dates from the third century; while other parts and phrases can be fixed at about the sixth century, with the exception of the *Hanc igitur,* which is even later. Nevertheless, it is one grand and over-ruling idea which has determined the whole train of thought we find here: it is that of the fellowship or communion of all Christians in God.

As Christ now makes ready to mount the Cross, the priest states the full purpose of the Sacrifice which is offered for the salvation of the Church militant on earth, and to the glory of the Church triumphant in heaven. He now calls forth and ranges round about the altar the whole company of baptized Christians, their leaders and exemplars at their head; he calls forth all who suffered and strove here below to lengthen the blessed shadow which the Cross casts over the sins of the world; and he calls, as well, on those

114

CANON MISSÆ

Finita Præfatione, Sacerdos extendens, elevam aliquantulum et jungens manus, elevansque ad cœlum oculos, et statim demittens, profunde inclinatus ante Altare, manibus super eo positis, dicit:

TE IGITUR, clementissime Pater, per Jesum Christum Filium tuum Dóminum nostrum, súpplices rogámus, ac pétimus, Osculatur Altare et, junctis manibus ante pectus, dicit: uti accépta hábeas, et benedícas, Signat ter super Hostiam et Calicem simul, dicens: hæc ✠ dona, hæc ✠ múnera, hæc ✠ sancta sacrificia illibáta, Extensis manibus prosequitur: in primis, quæ tibi offérimus pro Ecclésia tua sancta cathólica: quam pacificáre, custodire, adunáre, et régere dignéris toto orbe terrárum:

una cum fámulo tuo Papa nostro N. et Antístite nostro N. et ómnibus orthodóxis, atque cathólicæ, et apostólicæ fidei cultóribus.

Commemoratio pro vivis

MEMENTO, Dómine, famulórum, famularúmque tuárum N. et N. Jungir manus, orat aliquantulum pro quibus orare inténdit: deinde manibus exténsis prosequitur: et ómnium circumstántium, quorum tibi fides cógnita est, et nota devótio, pro quibus tibi offerimus: vel qui tibi ófferunt hoc sacrificium laudis, pro se, suisque ómnibus: pro redemptióne animárum suárum, pro spe salútis, et incolumitátis suæ: tibíque reddunt vota sua ætérno Deo, vivo et vero.

✠ Per Annum, ut infra 298

who are now sharers in that glory to which we look. In first place stands the glorious Virgin, Mary the Mother of God, the Consoler of Men. As a matter of fact, the whole Christian community (the word *familia* is actually used) is conceived of as being now assembled here where the sacrificial prayer is making into a present reality the rapidly approaching moment when, by transubstantiation, the whole substance of the offerings will become the whole substance of the Body and Blood of Christ Our Lord.

L ORD, all we stand here in Your sight, we Your witnesses throughout the world, united in the brotherhood of faith and of hope,

all we, Lord, who in Your holy will and grace are sons of the Church You so deeply love.

Here is Your Vicar who most fully bears in Your name, the burden and the care of all the churches;

here is Your flock; men good and bad, the strong of heart and those who are fearful; all are come together to await Your blessing.

And by their side stand those who even now do look upon Your face: here are Your apostles, Your martyrs, Your beloved, Your chosen ones.

In sacramental union, they are one with us; despite our failings and our sinfulness, they join to our offering the fellowship of the saints.

All we are here, agonizing Jesus, seeing You torn with the bitterness of unmerited pain and woe,

we are here in the certain hope that by Your word the bread and the wine we offer are made the earnest of our redemption.

Now, Lord, we pray that, just as in that final moment of Your earthly life You gazed in love on Mary and on John,

You will now turn Your face to Your whole church, standing with heart overflowing in love and supplication, beside the Cross whereon Your Sacrifice is wrought.

XX

This is My Body

THE ELEVATION OF THE HOST

Vain is every attempt to explain, on merely historical grounds, the signification of this high liturgical act which is the very culmination of the Mass. The Church says nothing of herself; but, hiding herself behind the Person of the Christ, uses no words, employs no gestures, but His own. The *Consecration* and the Supper are one. The Consecration reproduces and extends the mystic memorial of the Last Supper when Jesus, who was facing betrayal and death, freely offered his Body and His Blood for the redemption of mankind. In this lies the essence of the Mass as it has existed from the days of the early Christians; for the book of the Acts and the apostolic Letters offer more than one testimonial to its celebration. In the beginning, to this rite was joined that of the fraternal supper, the *Agapé* or love-feast of the community;[1] but out of respect for the holier rite, the connection between it and the Agapé was broken at about the end of the first century.

Christ, therefore, is seen to be the author of the form, the actions, the very words of the Consecration. In this moment, the priest quite literally becomes Christ Himself: his own personality is blotted out; it is absorbed in that of the everlasting Priest who is, at one time, the offered victim and the supreme officiant. For this reason it is Our Lord's own movements, as reported by the Gospel, which determine what the priest does: just as the Master did, the celebrant now raises his eyes on high; as Jesus blest the bread, so does he. (The genuflexion which the priest inserts here is no more than a personal mani-

festation of his adoration of God now sacramentally present.) The words, too, which the celebrant says are the very words used by Jesus—"those great and wondrous words," as St. Athanasius called them—those words which, in their simple directness, offer a contrast to the rich formularies wherein they are enshrined. It is as though God would show that He has no need for a multiplicity of verbiage.

Nevertheless, what we have in the liturgical formularies is no merely textual reproduction of the evangelical account: something has been added in the course of the centuries.[2] Such are certain adjectives, as those which describe the hands of Our Lord as *sanctas ac venerabiles* (holy and worthy of respect), or the word (inspired by Psalm 22:5) by which the chalice is called *praeclarum,* or glorious. None of these additions is of much importance.

Since the medieval period we find, in the midst of the consecratory formula for the wine, the words: *Mysterium fidei,* the mystery or sacrament of faith.[3] Their meaning is that here shines forth the essence of the Christian faith; for now *truly, really, substantially* (such is the Tridentine terminology), the bread and the wine are become the Body and the Blood of Jesus Christ.

It is because of the greatness of this mystery[4] that it has been so panoplied with solemnity. Especially has this been so since the twelfth century when heresy cast doubt upon the real presence. The thrice-rung bell, the clouds of incense, the lighting of a third

candle,[5]—all are tributes to the Holy Presence. Particularly does the Elevation affirm this Presence in a magnificent gesture which, at once, raises to heaven and shows to the whole congregation, the bread which has become the Body of Christ. Before bowing down in profound adoration, the devout soul looks up in the very fullness of faith and hope at the little host which veils the greatest of all mysteries.

HERE BEFORE YOUR FACE, devoutly I adore You:
My mind divests itself of all but You;
This bread on which I gaze, this bread raised now on high,
It is You, Yourself, Your very flesh: this I believe and trust.

As now, in silence, naught but You I see,
Grant me to cleave more firmly to my faith;
Subdue my will, my heart, my reason; and, by Your grace,
May all the love you've showered on me, flow back to You.

XXI

This is My Blood

THE ELEVATION OF THE CHALICE

It is not enough to adore God-made-man who is now present in the host. Nor are we to be satisfied by an entire acceptance of the mystery of transubstantiation. What must be done is to turn in full realization toward the action which now is being wrought at the altar. This is a purely sacrificial act, and it must generally be admitted that the wine evokes, in a more striking manner than does the bread, the force of the sacrificial act by recalling the blood so freely shed on Calvary's hill by the victor Victim. At this point, we are become witnesses of Christ's act of immolation. We are, as a matter of fact, more intimately united to it than are mere witnesses; for it is we ourselves who offer to the Father this lamb who now mystically sacrifices Himself: we are partakers, sharers, participants, in His act.

This puts us in touch with what has been, from time out of memory, recognized as being the core and the center of the oldest religious tradition. It is by the shedding of blood in reparation that man has ever appeased supernatural Power. In the days of old Israel every fault of whatsoever kind, be it one attaching moral or even merely ceremonial defilement, had to be blotted out in blood. *Sine sanguine non fit remissio:* without the shedding of blood, there is no forgiveness of sin.[1]

Yet it is evident that the mere sacrificial act of itself, unqualified by purpose, by supplicatory prayer, by participation, is of itself unavailing. "Is not this cup we bless," asks St. Paul, "a participation in Christ's blood?" (I Cor., 10:16). The words themselves by which the wine is consecrated are much more explicit than are those of the consecration of the bread, and they have the effect of indicating very forcibly that we are here concerned with a means of attachment between God and man, with a "New Covenant." Here again we confront the *mysterium fidei*, the mystery or sacrament of faith; it is by sharing in the Victim's offering that man can find pardon for his own sins.

Just as he did with the host, the priest lifts the chalice and shows it to the people, after he has blessed it. This is a more recent usage than the elevation of the host; for during the Middle Ages chalices were generally wider than those we use today, and hence more difficult to hold aloft in due reverence; but it is clear that the purpose of this elevation is a similar one: it is a tribute to the *Presence* of the Blood of Christ.

At this time we should join to the Life which is offered sacrificially on Calvary, our own life, by uniting in full oblation, for our own life is without meaning unless it be thus given to its Giver.

TRULY DO I BELIEVE that this Blood now offered in the Chalice
Is Your own, once given to the Father,
Truly the same that gushed forth 'neath scourge and lance,
Most truly the Blood that flows forever from Your wounds.

Grant, Crucified Jesus, that in its flowing
Your Blood may mingle with my own, unworthy though I am;
Grant that I, too, may give my life to God, and join
My sacrifice to Yours, my life thus being oned with Your own.

XXII

In Remembrance...

THE SUPPLICES

After the consecration of the bread and wine, Jesus said: *Haec quotiescumque feceritis, in mei memoriam facietis,* "As often as you do this, do it in remembrance of me." Therefore, doubtless already in the time of the Apostles, and in any case before the close of the second century, the Church had here inserted in the Liturgy a Memorial or Anamnesis (*Unde et memores . . .*), to which there were added, but shortly thereafter, two supplicatory prayers (*Supra quae propitio . . .* and *Supplices te rogamus . . .*). In the ensemble of these three prayers there is evident a grave sobriety in which are recognized the accents of primitive Christianity.

To what does this Memorial or Anamnesis have reference? Certainly to the Passion,[1] for that it is which the Oblation of the Supper evokes. And it is for this reason that the celebrant now signs Host and Chalice with the Cross, and that according to some particular liturgical uses,[2] he here extends his arms in cross-like fashion. ". . . it is the Lord's death that you are heralding," St. Paul has told us, "whenever you eat this bread and drink this cup . . ." (I Cor., 11:26). This is then certainly a recalling of His death; but it recalls, as well, Christ's Resurrection and His glorious Ascension. Therefore in the anamnesis we have a sort of resumé or summing-up of the whole Mass: it underlines the whole meaning of the Mass that it may the more fully reveal it.

The Oblata upon which we begged God's blessing are now become one with "that pure, holy, unspotted Oblation, the sacred bread of life everlasting, the cup of redemption." We turn to God and are bold to say that these gifts can now be received by Him; for they are no longer unworthy of Him. And did He not, aforetime, receive the sacrifices of Abel, of Abraham, and of Melchisedech, all of which were no more than types or figures of His Son's sacrifice? Thus does the past indicate what is to be.

Now bowing low in supplication, the priest begs of the Almighty Lord that He would give to us, in the Eucharistic Communion which we are later to share, that Christ whom we have here set forth in His sight. This is the intent of the prayer which begins with the word *Supplices.* Of this most meaningful and mysterious prayer Innocent III remarked that human understanding can scarce apprehend its full significance. Before the face of God's ineffable Majesty, the only acceptable Offering is laid upon the heavenly Altar, and the angelic liturgy completes what human worship had begun: thus is the Sacrifice made on earth consummated in heaven.

And we may feel assured that, if we have but taken thought to entrust them to Him, it is our hopes and our fears, the best part of our very selves, which the Sacred Victim now carries into the Father's Heart.

HOW GREAT had been my joy
Had I been one among the throngs
That gathered round the Lake while Jesus spoke!

What chill had struck my soul had I been there,
When from the tomb, responding to His simple call,
The answering Lazarus came forth!

Would not His words have burned within my breast
Had I been there, when at the Table, long ago,
He first gave thanks and broke the Holy Bread?

Would not my heart have cracked in tears and pain
Had I stood near His Cross, on Calvary's hill,
With Magdalene, Our Lady, and St. John?

And, had I seen, that Easter morn,
The rollèd stone, the empty tomb,
Would not my soul have overflowed in hope new born?

But hearken now, my soul: in all these words and acts,
Even in prayers that your distraction failed to hear,
In all are now, by mystic drama here enacted,
The saving floods, unfathomed yet, of your Redemption!

Your kneeling at this Altar is no empty form;
Love grips you here: your life's the price of yielding.
Your dry roots now unveil; and let them watered be
While Jesus wraps you in the mantle of His blood.

XXIII

Our Dead and We Sinners

THE COMMEMORATION OF THE DEAD

Is it for ourselves that we are offering this Sacrifice? It can never be too often repeated that the Mass is rooted in fellowship, in a union with Christ the Son of God, and with men, our brethren. At the very beginning of Mass, by the Collect, and later, by the formularies preparatory to the Consecration, we were reminded of this; and now again two further intercessory prayers re-enforce the will which should be in us for brotherly union.

Before Christ was raised aloft in the Elevation, the Church militant and the Church triumphant were assembled around the Cross; but the Liturgy now pauses to consider the sorrowing Church as prayer is offered for the dead and for sinners.

Prayer for the dead is of great antiquity. It was known to the Synagogue; and St. John Chrysostom assures us that the tradition has passed to us directly from the Apostles. Nevertheless, the actual *Commemoration* of the dead, as we now have it, is like the other Commemorations something of late introduction into the Mass. It is not found in manuscripts of as late as the eleventh century. We may ask then why it was placed here at a point of such importance in the ceremony? The Fathers of the Church had already given the reason; and it is St. Cyril of Jerusalem who tells us that we ought pray for those in greatest need just when our prayer is most efficacious. Such indeed are those who, although they have passed death's Portal, still await the final revelation of refreshment, light, and peace.

The mere mention of the Souls in Purgatory should provoke us to thought of ourselves, for our own death is but a thing delayed; and it is we who are the future tenants in that state of purgation. It is for this reason that the celebrant passes quickly from the dead to us; and he fervently begs the divine loving kindness for us who are sinners (*nobis quoque peccatoribus*), in words so simple and direct as to indicate the antiquity of the tradition upon which they rest.

And, as he had done before the Consecration at the Commemoration of the Living, the celebrant calls again for the aid of intercessors, and he names here another group of saints and martyrs.[1] They are witnesses and pledges of the glory that shall be ours. Thus for the third time, and in a most definitive manner, do we find evoked that grand and wondrous reality of Christian faith, the doctrine of the Communion of Saints, which is our fellowship with the blessed.

NOW THAT MY PRAYER is no longer my prayer alone, but has been voiced by the divine lips of Your Crucified Son,

allow me, my Lord, in trusting confidence to put before You the plight of my brethren in You, my brethren who yet walk in the night of this mortal life:

for all whom I love; for those whom I have scarce loved at all but now join together in my heart's remembrance;

for the long generations of Christians whose prayers have been, in earlier days, borne up to You, even as now mine are;

for those who are dead, as I myself shall one day be; for those whose present faults bespeak their need of atonement's sharpest anguish;

for all with whom I soon shall be united; for all whose only hope is fixed upon Your holy Cross;

for all I beg Your saving Grace, for them and for myself. And grant, my Lord, that the offering of Your blood may pledge assuagement of that death and trial which are the wages of my sin.

XXIV

Thanksgiving

THE LITTLE ELEVATION

The Canon of the Mass here comes to its term. The few phrases which now bring to a close the long series of prayers introduced by the Preface are simple in their appearance; but, as is generally true in the liturgy, they are all the more weighty in their significance. In the first of these, which opens with the words *Per quem . . .*, we say to the Lord: "It is in Christ that You have given enduring life to all these good things; in Him that You have made them holy and useful; in Him that You bless them and give them to us." Are we to look upon this formulary as a mere resumé of the Canon, designed to bring it to a formal end? Or is it rather the remnant of some antique blessing, directed not alone to the bread and the wine, but as well to milk and honey, to the fruit of the vine, or to the new-born lambs, or to the yield of the new bean crop? It is at just this point in the rite that on Holy Thursday there is still hallowed the oil with which the sick are anointed.[1] In any case, there is no mystery about the *meaning* of this formulary. The result of the mediation of the Incarnate God, who offers Himself for the salvation of the whole world, is that the divine creative power is ever renewing holiness, grace, and love in all God has made.

By a special liturgical act the priest now appropriately expresses God's having made holy, having raised above their natural state, the things of created existence. This act is called the *Little* (or *Minor*) *Elevation*.[2] The celebrant raises host and chalice slightly as he begins the formulary, *Per ipsum . . .*[3] In the early Church this was the only Elevation in the Mass; for, as we know, the Elevation at the Consecration dates only from the Middle Ages.

This Elevation is even more full of meaning than is the Great (or Major) Elevation; but its intent is different. It is not now to the people that the Oblata are presented: they are here held aloft to God, for the bread and the wine are become the Body and the Blood of His divine Son.

In the full sense of the term, and more expressly than are any of the prayers which precede the Consecration, this liturgical act is a *Thanksgiving*. The words which the priest says make this clear: *Per ipsum . . .* "Through Whom (i.e., Christ), by Whom, and with Whom, in the unity of the Holy Ghost, all honor and glory be unto You, O Father Almighty, world without end." It is through Christ our Mediator, in union with Him, and in a sense absorbed or incorporated in Him, that we His ransomed ones will partake with all His creation in the blessed praise of the Holy Trinity for ever. The *Amen* which closes this sublime prayer is without doubt the most significant Amen in the entire course of the Mass. This was anciently the only time that Amen was said during the old Canon; and here the word is used in its most complete and extensive sense. Let us therefore say it together, with heart-felt fervor: "So be it."

134

NOW IS ALL CREATION ransomèd, and there rests upon us the joy of unimaginable promise!

This is a promise of everlasting renewal: the seven ages of creation are refreshingly re-enacted!

All now is purified, truth reigns again, and the world around me is become once more as it was in the beginning; the heart broken by sorrow is healed in love.

A wheaten host, a cup of wine, raised to the Incarnate God in sacrificial offering, bespeak the re-awakening of all terrestrial things to their destined glory; and the marvelous glad light of the Trinity puts the darksome night to flight.

In a sacramental gesture which is beyond my power to understand, I raise up and offer to You, my Lord, all that is good; for all this is Your creation and belongs not to me, but to You alone;

and I know that by this sacrament there is brought to pass my salvation, destined from the beginning of time and perduring for ever.

Grant that I may be open to all the instrumentalities of Your Grace which this fleeting world offers in the days of my sojourning here;

make holy, with Your blessing, all that I am and might wish to be, all that I have, and all that I would surrender in the Love of Christ.

Grant, too, that I may respond in my heart with fitting joyousness to all Your boundless Love which dowers its gifts upon me!

XXV

The Pater Noster

THE LORD'S PRAYER

The last act of the liturgical drama now begins; this fifth act is the conclusion of all. I have *prayed;* I have *listened to the Word;* I have made my *offering;* I have *joined in the Sacrifice;* now it is my turn to *receive.* At the sacrificial table I shall be united in Communion with Jesus.

The course of the liturgy enters upon this its last phase in a somewhat unexpected manner. There is first said a very touching and most ancient formulary (one alluded to already in the fourth century by St. Jerome), which asserts that were it not for the express command of Our Lord we should by no means presume to utter what we are about to say. This introduction is recited by the celebrating priest with his hands joined in a way which symbolizes a strong sense of unity—unity with God in Christ, unity, as well, with our brethren. Then he extends his hands, and solemnly says the *Our Father,* in which he may be joined by the congregation.[1] This is the Lord's own prayer, the prayer that encompasses all others. St. Luke has given us an account (11:2–4) of how Jesus, but a short time before He suffered, taught this prayer to His disciples in response to their request: "Lord, teach us how to pray." Was this from a balcony in Ephrem or on the slopes of Mt. Olivet? Was it a prayer He had already used after the Sermon on the Mount, as St. Matthew's text suggests (6:9–13)? There cannot be any doubt that it expresses the heart of Our Lord's Gospel: this prayer is His spiritual legacy to us. The custom of reciting the *Pater* at the Eucharist is of great antiquity, and it may be of even apostolic origin: many are the allusions made to this custom in the writings of the old Church Fathers, and St. Augustine regarded it as something long established in his own time. In the sixth century St. Gregory the Great, while pope, decreed that this prayer should be said just prior to the Communion, and he was surely guided by high inspiration and profound insight in this decision. What, after all, is the Holy Communion but the very sacrament of unity? And in preparation for it what is more desired than the charity or love of God and of our fellow men which the *Pater* arouses in us?

Before we partake of the Body of Christ it is fitting that we share in His spirit.

138

I WOULD, my Lord, say no longer distractedly or in some routine fashion the prayer which You have taught me. This is the prayer said, down the centuries, by countless numbers of Your followers. They have never grown tired of obeying Your injunction to repeat it. I would now say it slowly and with as much awareness and consideration as though I were listening when You first taught men its words.

You tell me that God is my Father, not only my Master and my King; that He shows Himself to me not as the Mighty God upon whose face no man may gaze, not as the God of hosts, terrifying in the majesty of His justice; but rather as the Father who has raised me to sonship with You; making me an heir to His kingdom; that, despite His power and His glory I may confidently rely on His love of me.

Father, I pray You to keep us ever in Your sight; be as near to us on earth as You are to those who have entered into Your heavenly kingdom. Be with me by the bright light of Your glory in my soul; rule my spirit; and make my heart overflow with love. Be with me in Your power, establishing the kingdom of Your justice. Be with me in the open showing to me of Your will, so that I may strive joyously to accomplish it.

I ask You to sustain me in this life for as long as You will, and to grant me to earn my bread. Each day may I act with complete trust in Your providential care of me, and may I thus eat the bread of brotherhood, sharing with my fellows not only the bread which nourishes the body, but that upon which the soul is fed as well; for it is that Living Bread come down from heaven which alone can satisfy our hunger.

I ask You, once more, to forgive me all that I have done amiss; for the weight of my transgressions is more than I can bear. In the face of Your loving kindness to me, may I ever remember to conform my own conduct to it; may I be generous, ready to forgive others with brotherly love, just as You are to all of us.

Grant that temptation in the battles of my daily life may never be too much for my puny strength, as I go from one mortal trial to another; spare me those heavy trials which break the spirit, those troubles which distress the heart; and do not deliver me over to the enemy who dwells in my own evil inclinations. Father, now as the Blood of Your Son is about to bring me Your grace, Father, I beg You to have mercy upon me!

XXVI

The Broken Bread

THE BREAKING OF THE HOST

After He had broken bread, the bread which He had blessed and made holy, Jesus said to His disciples: "Take and eat." The Holy Communion is thus indicated to be an integral part of the Mass, and the logical and indispensable completion of the Consecration. (It is, therefore, a mistake to sunder them by seeking, without real necessity, to communicate apart from Mass, or to withdraw from the progress of the liturgical action of the Mass into selfishly personal meditation as though one could thus better attain the union with Christ which Mass affords!)

Long ago in Israel, under the Old Law, "the Feast of the Most High" was a part of sacrificial worship, and the participants ate of the victim after some parts of it had been burned upon the altar, and the fumes had been wafted on high: thus to have joined in the divine feast by accepting the sacred' aliments was an act pleasing to Almighty God. To an even greater extent, under the New Law, the Sacred Banquet possesses a power to unite its participants to God. Has not Christ Himself said, "My flesh is real food, my blood is real drink"? (John 6:56). At the Last Supper, the Apostles assuredly ate the bread and drank the wine the Master had blessed; in Apostolic times, the baptized Christians gathered together in the *Agapé,* which was at once a supper of fraternal love and of liturgical communion. Even later on, when the Supper and the Communion were no longer joined together, it was customary to keep up the lively remembrance of the banquet.[1] In our own time we have perhaps lost this feeling of sharing in a Common Supper, despite the fact that such a realization expresses so strikingly the concept of that brotherly union in God which is so necessary to the fruitful reception of the Holy Sacrament. Yet even now, the actions and the words of the priest awake in our hearts inspiring echoes of past usage.

First the celebrant, in the words of a very old prayer, takes up again and develops further the idea on which the *Pater* had closed: he recalls in the *Libera nos* that it is by Christ that we are delivered.[2] The priest then raises the Host and breaks it into two parts, and after placing one of the two halves on the paten, he breaks off a small portion of the other and puts it into the chalice. These three acts of the *Fraction* are full of significance. The divided host represents the bread broken at the Last Supper (the Jews always broke, and never *cut*, their bread): it was in the act of breaking bread that the Risen Lord was made known to the disciples at Emmaus. According to the mystical interpretation devised in the Middle Ages, this represents the Body of Christ being broken during His Passion; but, above all, by this act is figured the distribution of His sacramental Body to His brethren. The particle set on one side recalls the old rite of the *Sancta;* a particle consecrated at a previous Mass used always be reserved until this time by way of enforcing the idea that the Mass is one; it is a perpetuation of the Mass said before, and it is continued by the Mass which will follow.[3] And, finally, the little

piece which is dropped into the Chalice, according to a rite which goes back to the fourth century, is a symbol of the Body and Blood of the Risen Lord united as a pledge of our own resurrection to everlasting life. Others explain it as an affirmation of the perfect union in Christ of divine and human nature. However, it has also been regarded at all times as a representation of the manner in which everyone of us is conjoined to our brethren within the bosom of the Church: we are each part of the other, just as this little particle of Bread dissolves in the Wine.

MY LORD, this is the very bread that was broken by You at the Last Supper, and was there given by Your own hands to Your apostles; this is the bread that Your martyrs shared, one with another, before they were themselves crushed and broken by the teeth of wild beasts as the wheat is crushed under the grindstone;

this is the bread partaken of by the long line of Your saints which stretches from age to age in an unending union of love and fellowship;

this is the same bread which, even now, is being renewed everywhere upon the earth in a great Mass that never ends.

Grant, therefore, that I may so receive this living bread as to recall that I am not alone, but am joined in real fellowship with all Your followers;

grant, O Lord Christ, that just as You give Yourself in every least morsel of this bread, grant that I may share Your own love for those who know You and for those who know You not;

grant that I may be thus ever more firmly linked to redeemed humanity, to all who are ransomed by Your Blood, that so I may fulfill the purpose for which You made Your Sacrifice.

XXVII

In the Blood of the Lamb

THE AGNUS DEI

"Sheep led away to the slaughter-house, lamb that stands dumb while it is shorn; no word from him." It was thus that the prophet Isaias, in a well-known passage (53:7), proclaimed the Messiah; and the Baptist took up this strain when he cried out, at the coming of Jesus: "Look, this is the Lamb of God; look, this is he who takes away the sin of the world" (John 1:29).

Again does the liturgy recur to the symbolism of the lamb in placing upon our lips a three-fold plea in the words of the *Agnus Dei*. These invocations are in the tradition set for the children of old Israel by Moses when he required that they mark the post of their doors with the blood of a lamb on that far-off paschal night while they were yet in Egypt. It was in this sign that they were spared by the Lord's Angel.

From the viewpoint of liturgiological history, it seems that the *Agnus Dei* is either the remnant of, or a substitute for, some old litany formerly sung while the consecrated Bread was being broken in preparation for its distribution among the attendants at Mass. This was sometimes a very protracted ceremony. The invocation here of the Lamb of God arose at first in the Eastern Church, and it was a Syrian pope, St. Sergius I, who authoritatively established the custom at Rome, toward the close of the seventh century. The meaning of the three straight-forward pleas to the Lamb of God is evident. Was not Israel protected by the paschal lamb; and is not the Lamb that is sacrificed the pledge of the reconciliation, thus cemented, of man with God?

It is, however, in the final words of this three-fold invocation that we may precisely discern how the love of God is found; for whereas to the first and second cries of *Agnus Dei* the response is "have mercy upon us," the plea that follows the final invocation is "grant us peace." It is on the heels of these words that the celebrant now prays that the Church may be brought to peace and unity; and here it is that, in solemn Masses, there takes place the lovely rite of the *Pax*. The giving of the kiss of peace is rooted in the practice of Our Lord and His apostles; it was thought by the primitive Christians to be something of prime importance; and it is a fault in Christians of our own time that they fail to observe it.

Once more do the words and acts prescribed by the liturgy underline that special lesson which the Mass tirelessly teaches: if we sincerely desire that God keep us in that peace which is an assurance of His love, then must we love one another!

146

MY LORD, there is but one sign by which You shall know me when You come in judgment, seated on the clouds of heaven and surrounded by the blinding light of Your glory in which all hidden things will lie revealed.

That sign will then be of even greater avail against the angels of divine wrath than were the marked door-posts of Israel;

it is the sign of which we read in the Apocalypse that Your servants bear it on their faces as it were a seal of their devotion to You;

it is the sign of Your loving kindness, known indeed to me, even though my heart does not wholly own it:

it is the mark and sign of the Lamb, the mark by which Your Blood will blot out forever all the hatred and spiritual unrest seated in my heart;

it is the sign of peace, of shared pardon, of brotherly affection; the sign of Your own love for us shared in by every one of us.

Ah, grant me, my Lord, a longing for this sign, that I may be marked with it, ineffaceably, in the innermost depth of my soul;

and grant that in the strength of Your sign, the mark of the Lamb, I may gain for You the whole world, that world which You have promised to those who are gentle and forbearing.

XXVIII

The Celebrant's Communion

THE PRIEST RECEIVES THE HOLY COMMUNION

It is now that the celebrant makes ready to partake of the Communion, by saying two prayers which are full of fervor. In one he begs that Christ, the giver of life, will grant salvation to His servant and join him to Himself; in the other he professes his own deep unworthiness in the face of this unthought of gift, and he begs that it may not work to his condemnation.[1] Although these prayers are most beautiful, they are rather subjective in tone and they do not belong to the main line of thought in the Mass which is, as we know, the enforcement of that primary intention that the whole Christian family be drawn together and associated one with another in the liturgical action. They are prayers of private piety, as their relatively recent introduction into the Ordinary demonstrates; they date from only about the tenth century.[2] Nevertheless, they afford each one of us an opportunity to test within his own individual selfhood that will for a general union, a shared participation, which underlies the whole Mass.

The Communion of the celebrating priest is an indispensable and essential part of every Mass. So necessary is it that if, through some unforeseen occurrence, the celebrant should be unable to communicate, another priest must take his place as soon as possible, and must consume the Sacred Elements in his stead. What sort of sacrifice would that be which was left incomplete? It is with the celebrant and, as it were, beside him, that each one of us ought fulfill the Sacrifice! The priest takes our place; he sacrifices for us. Do not the words which he pronounces express the very sentiments which rise up from the deep places of our own hearts?

In confession of our unworthiness we recall what was said by the centurion at Capharnaum; in words of gratitude we declare our wonder before these fruitful gifts of God; in words of confidence we mark the fulfillment of our worship: all unworthy as I am, I partake of everlasting life in sharing the Body and the Blood of Christ, the everliving God . . .

I AM ABASED in Your sight as my soul hungers and thirsts for You;

my whole being awaits You in the silent stillness in which You come to me.

Never before have I so realized my unworthiness, my wretched unfitness—it is truly boundless;

never before has the intolerable sense of this unworthiness pressed so heavily upon me;

never before have I seen so clearly the truth that of myself I am nothing, that of myself I am powerless:

it is therefore in an entire recognition of my own insignificance that I kneel before You in my deep distress and tear from myself the veils of vain pretense;

for it is to You alone that I do wholly trust myself: I know that You will not cast me off.

I believe that by Your coming to me You will grant me strength and fullness of life.

I believe that, in Your Word, whatever is broken within me will be healed, whatever is unclean will be made again pure.

I believe that in this Host and in that Cup You are truly present— my God, it is with every energy of my soul that I trust and believe in You!

XXIX

The Communion of the People

THE CONGREGATION

APPROACH THE HOLY TABLE

It is now that, in their turn, the assistants at Mass come to receive their God, to be united to Him; for to communicate is more than merely to receive. At first the distribution of the Sacred Elements was done at the same table where the *Agapé*[1] had been held, and the clergy gave them to those who were about the table; but after the fourth century it was the congregation which went solemnly toward the altar, that "Holy Table" whose very name recalls the Table of the Last Supper. In primitive times, the consecrated Bread was put into the palm of the communicant's hand, and in the mind of the early Fathers this signified the sanctification of the human senses. Then the faithful would drink, in turn, from a common cup. Communion under the two kinds—by reception of both bread and wine—is even yet the rule among the Greeks; and it persisted widely in the West until about the twelfth century, not being, in fact, officially suppressed until the action of the Council of Constance in 1418.[2]

From about the thirteenth century it became customary for the communicants to say the *Confiteor* before receiving the holy sacrament, and the priest gave the absolution,

Misereatur . . . and *Indulgentiam* . . . in the same form as had already been used at the beginning of the Mass. This repetition has been eliminated by the new rubrics: and, nowadays, the priest, after having received the Precious Blood, lifts up one of the small hosts from the paten or ciborium and, first saying, "Behold the Lamb of God . . ." (to which the communicants respond, "O Lord, I am not worthy . . ."), he proceeds at once to communicate the server and the others in attendance who come forward. During solemn Masses, it is at this point that the Communion Anthem is sung. As in the case of the *Introït*, it may be followed by appropriate verses of the Psalm from which it is taken or by some choral voluntary having reference to Our Lord in the Blessed Sacrament.

Kneeling and in turn, we now receive into our mouths the Bread of Life.[3] As he administers the host to each communicant, the celebrant says, *"The Body of Christ,"* to which the reply is made, *"Amen."* [4] It is, indeed, by these words that I know my time of waiting to be over, for my hope is now made into a reality which fulfills the deepest needs of my faith and my love.

154

THERE IS NEITHER SPEECH nor language—not even the language by which heart speaks to heart—fit to express all that I would now say; my joy is beyond speech.

I feel the light of Your Face shining upon me, my innermost being responds to the warmth of Your love;

You are mine, and I am Yours, wholly made one in this Sacrament: my soul worships You in stillness.

No merely human sense of gratitude even begins to take account of this gift so far above the feebleness of human insight;

no love can ever equal the Love which caused You to make Your sacrifice;

every proffered gift, every good intent, when looked at in the light of Your example and of Your offering of Yourself, is seen to be as naught.

Therefore, my Lord, what is there that I can offer You? What can I find to say to You? It is only Yourself that is worthy of You; Yourself whom I have now received in the silence of my soul.

I would now ask You, as I look back to that day of my childhood when I innocently bade You welcome in the very first of my Communions,

I would now ask You that You make me to be what it is You wish me to be, that You keep me as You would have me be;

I ask that I may share in Your own Sacrifice, and that You will be with me as I carry my Cross, as I go from sorrow to joy, from hope to fear;

I ask You to live within my soul, to possess me wholly and to remain the moving force in all that I shall do throughout my life. My God, bear me as a child in Your arms.

XXX

In the Hand of God

THE BLESSING

The Communion over, the Mass seems to come to a close all at once; and there are some who have felt disturbed by this: they would have wished for more time in which to prolong their personal acts of devotion. It is true that the thankful prayers of a soul just visited by Christ are among the very best prayers that can be offered to God. The Church indeed counsels us to make such prayers at this time. Nevertheless, it seemed to the early Christians that the whole Mass was a continued *thanksgiving*, and that after having been made holy by the presence of the sacramental body within himself, the individual Christian could best prolong that thanksgiving by his practice of the love of his fellow men, by the acceptance of the joys and the sorrows of his own lot, by maintaining his devotional fervor.

There are two levels of meaning indicated by the prayers which are said after the Communion. In the first prayers we ask that God will grant that His gifts may do their destined work in us by keeping us in purity of life; by assuring, as one prayer movingly puts it, that what we have received in the time of mortality, may endure in our souls as an everlasting renewal of life. On the whole, this sums up the meaning of the *Ablution Prayers* which, for about thirteen hundred years, have been said while the priest cleanses the traces of the holy Body and Blood which may chance to remain on his own lips or fingers, or in the chalice. Such, also, is the signification of the *Postcommunion,* a venerable companion prayer to

the *Collect* and the *Prayer over the Oblations*. It, too, varies with the Mass which is being said. This prayer states in definite terms our wish that the fruits of the Sacrifice may remain in us. Herein lies the conclusion of the act of receiving the Holy Communion.

However, these perspectives are somewhat enlarged by four liturgical acts which now take place. Just as the Mass is drawing to its end, and we are about to take up the work of our daily lives in the midst of cares and danger, the Church reminds us that we must live under the Hand of God, and that as a matter of fact it is under His Hand that we will be guided and protected. In this way the whole essence of the Mass will be, in a sense, incorporated into our being and continued in our daily lives. The *Oratio super populum,* or Prayer said over the people (which is now in use only on week-days from Ash Wednesday until the Wednesday of Holy Week), is of Oriental institution, and it recalls to each one of us, as we listen to its clauses of blessing, that we are all God's children. The *Ite Missa est,* or formulary of dismissal, can be explained as being a solemn announcement of the conclusion of the service, but it also gives notice that our individual service of God is but beginning: the word *missio* can be rendered not only as "dismissal," but also as "mission."[1] By the *Placeat* (which Pius V caused to be inserted in his Missal in the sixteenth century) we are bidden to a realization of the omnipresent Triune God in whose name the final *Blessing* [2] is now invoked upon us. In a beautiful

liturgical gesture, the celebrant raises his hands on high as though he would draw down from heaven the Grace which now goes forth with us to guard and to guide us. In earlier days this benediction was thought to be so solemn and so important an act that it was only the bishop who could exercise it until as late as the eleventh century.

MY LORD, I beg that You will keep alive in the depths of my heart the thought of this Mass at which I have assisted: grant that I may not look upon it as just another passing hour in a busy life; for it is truly a means by which Your Grace has come to me, and it has given me an opportunity to unite myself more intimately to You.

Do not cast me off, but grant that I may know Your guiding hand to be ever with me: just as in those far-off days You led Your chosen people by the sign of the cloud, so now I beg that You will guide and sustain me by keeping Your presence constantly alive in my thoughts.

And grant that I myself may never turn aside from You: make me always mindful that You are ever present to me as the One reality that no man can overlook. I wish always to seek and to find Your purpose for me in the outward events of my life as well as in those secret encounters whereby I feel my destiny to be shaped.

I beg that my life may be nourished by faith, motivated by love, enlightened by hope, so that I may meet both happiness and trials without losing my sense of reliance upon You; grant that Your Grace may increase within me, and around me, so that all my life may be a prolongation of this Mass and of my union with You.

Postlude

IN RECOLLECTION

One of the most vivid pictures in the Gospels, deeply etched in the heart of the meditative Christian, is that in which we see Our Lady and St. John standing beside the Cross while Mary Magdalene kneels before it. It is a scene upon which Christian artists have loved to linger: many are the rood screens or jubes, particularly in our older churches, which depict these figures. Countless, too, are the representations of this climactic moment in the history of mankind's redemption made to adorn the opening of the Canon as painted in illuminated manuscripts or engraved for the sumptuously printed Missals of a later age.

There is, surely, a valuable lesson for us here: we who have been at Mass have assisted again at Calvary; we have climbed once more that mountain of myrrh, that hill of incense (*Vadam ad montem myrrhae, ad collem thuris*, as the Church sings in one of the Vesper antiphons on the feast of the Compassion of Our Lady). Having ascended into the holy place, is it not fitting that we linger for a few moments in prayerful recollection? For this reason, the Church counsels her ministers to give thanks after Mass; and our Missals contain prayers especially designed to this end, one being the beautiful Canticle from the Book of Daniel which the three youths sang in the fiery furnace. The ages of faith have added other prayers; and we find, also in the Missal, a rich collection of indulgenced selections suited to varying moods. One is ascribed to St. Thomas Aquinas, another to St. Bonaventura. The *Adoro te*, the *Anima Christi*, the well-known *Prayer before the Crucifix*, and the touching *Obsecro te* are among them, as well. The prologue to the Fourth Gospel, which, formerly, was said at the end of Mass (by a simple priest at the altar, and by a bishop as he went in procession from the holy table to his throne), is another most suitable prayer for this time.

We, nowadays, have a more compelling reason to linger than did the first followers of Our Lord; for those who stood on Calvary's hill on the first Good Friday were keeping sad vigil beside their dead Master, whereas we have the joyous privilege of remaining to kneel in adoration before the most glorious Lord of Life. Jesus, as we know, is present not only at the Mass or in the actual moment of sacramental communion: in that sacred tent of meeting which we call the Tabernacle. He always abides, in a special sense, in our churches, ever interceding for us with the Father.

Shall we not be wise if, instead of hastily rushing forth at the conclusion of Mass, we stay a little longer in profound adoration of the mystery of the Eucharist, in heartfelt gratitude for the graces we have been given, in sincere petition for the help we need before we resume our work in the world and, as St. Paul suggests to us, take up again the task of winning it to Christ our Lord?

As NOW, once more, I walk the path of daily life,
Again take up its tasks and duties vexing,
True Light of Light, I call on You for light;
Increate Word; Reason for all being and all becoming:

No more than earthly life can flourish sunless
Could I, lacking You, live without the strength You impart;
As the moon of the sun, I am no more than a feeble reflection
Of Glory's provident care inspiring my least flicker of life.

I call upon You in the Majesty of Your Justice;
In You alone shall I find lasting Truth;
From You do I draw undying draughts of Hope,
Watering me with Grace that woos me to know Your Love.

Grant, Word of God, that my strivings may mirror
That unthought of reflection You will me to be;
Grant, that shown by my acts, fulfilled in my heart,
There may shine forth the pure Light of You I dimly discern in the dark.

It is You alone who can answer my questing,
My wish to know why and how this can be;
Yours alone is true knowledge of life:
Speak to my faith when I languish in doubt.

Grant me, O Word my Brother, born of a Virgin Mother,
Sharing with me life's sorrows and anguished end,
Grant me, when trustingly I kneel in Your sight,
Grant me to know that in You rests the answer to all that I seek.

Teach me how Majesty put on Mercy's robe
And bridged by the Cross the great chasm that set us apart:
May Your Blood be not shed in vain; save me, my God;
Let the Word of Your Love resound in my heart.

English Text of the Major Mass Prayers

The Kyrie

Lord, have mercy. (*thrice*)
Christ, have mercy. (*thrice*)
Lord, have mercy. (*thrice*)

The Gloria in Excelsis

Glory to God in the highest.
And on earth peace to men of good will.*
We praise You. We bless You. We worship You.
    We glorify You.*
We give You thanks for Your great glory.*
Lord God, heavenly King, God the Father Almighty.*
Lord Jesus Christ, the only-begotten Son.*
Lord God, Lamb of God, Son of the Father.*
You, Who take away the sins of the world,*
    have mercy on us.*
You, Who take away the sins of the world,*
    receive our prayer.*
You, Who sit at the right hand of the Father,*
    have mercy on us.*
For You alone are holy.*
You alone are Lord.*
You alone, O Jesus Christ, are most high,*
With the Holy Spirit, in the glory of God the Father. Amen.

The Credo

I believe in one God.
The Father Almighty, Maker of heaven and earth,*
  and of all things visible and invisible.*
And I believe in one Lord, Jesus Christ,*
  the only-begotten Son of God.
Born of the Father before all ages.*
God of God, Light of Light, true God of true God.*
Begotten, not made,*
  of one substance with the Father.*
By Whom all things were made.*
Who for us men and for our salvation came down from
  heaven.*
And He became flesh by the Holy Spirit of the Virgin Mary: *
  and was made man.*
He was also crucified for us,*
  suffered under Pontius Pilate, and was buried.*
And on the third day He rose again, according to the
  Scriptures.*
He ascended into heaven and sits at the right hand of
  the Father.*
He will come again in glory to judge the living and the dead.*
And of His kingdom there will be no end.*
And I believe in the Holy Spirit, the Lord and Giver
  of life,*
  Who proceeds from the Father and the Son.*
Who together with the Father and the Son is adored and
  glorified,*
  and Who spoke through the prophets.*
And one holy, catholic, and apostolic Church.*
I confess one baptism for the forgiveness of sins.*
And I await the resurrection of the dead.*
And the life of the world to come. Amen.

The Sanctus

Holy, Holy, Holy Lord God of hosts.*
Heaven and earth are filled with Your glory.*
Hosanna in the highest.*
Blessed is He Who comes in the name of the Lord.*
Hosanna in the highest.

The Pater Noster

Let us pray: Taught by our Savior's command and formed
    by the word of God, we dare to say:

Our Father, Who art in heaven,*
    hallowed be Thy name; *
Thy kingdom come; *
Thy will be done on earth as it is in heaven.*
Give us this day our daily bread; *
    and forgive us our trespasses *
    as we forgive those who trespass against us; *
    and lead us not into temptation,*
    but deliver us from evil.*
Amen.

The Agnus Dei

Lamb of God, Who take away the sins of the world,*
    have mercy on us.*
Lamb of God, Who take away the sins of the world,*
    have mercy on us.*
Lamb of God, Who take away the sins of the world,*
    grant us peace.
(In Requiem Masses: . . . grant them rest . . . grant them rest . . .
    grant them eternal rest.)

Translator's Annotations

The repeated assertion of Edmund Bishop [1] that the Liturgy cannot be fully understood apart from a knowledge of its historical background is in no need of justification to the thoughtful student. But those whose preoccupations have not disposed them to consider the subject in the light of history might be convinced of the validity of this opinion by either a careful backward glance or a searching look about them.

If we look back at primitive forms in Christian worship, we may observe that what is sometimes vaunted as being a desirable kind of "simplicity," to be sought after, is often due "not so much to the inwardness or spirituality of the new religion doctrinally, as to its crudeness and incapacity artistically." [2] And, if we choose to make our focal point the more elaborate forms characteristic of certain periods in later Christian history, we will find ourselves open to the sharp reminders of such as Père Bouyer or M. Cingria that (as the latter has said) sumptuousness and luxuriance often resulted in a state of affairs tending to obscure rather than to emphasize the end sought. [3] The highest sacred art—and liturgical observance is the union of all sacred arts—is perhaps at its best, they seem to suggest, when it is somewhat transparent, when it does not attempt to exhaust its subject, when it reveals rather by suggestion than by an overcareful attempt to spell out all that it would evoke. [4]

Yet, historicism and archaeology are not the answers, no more than is didacticism; and it is not in a mere echoing of the past that we are likely to find the best solution to the problems which beset every age. The notion, to which so gifted a writer as Joris-Karl Huysmans made his great talent subservient, that only in a specific form of architecture was the Christian vision embodied, that only in a limited kind of church music does the Spirit truly speak, is the distortion of a more universal truth than he allowed of. No less a distortion is *the classic rage* which, as Cardinal Newman thought, [5] bound even so generous a mind as that of the great Fénelon. Almost two thousand years of Catholic tradition belie any system which would too rigorously confine liturgical expression to any one of the almost innumerable forms in which it has found an outlet. An underlying and unifying sense is to be looked for otherwhere; and, just as C. C. Clifford remarked in one of his unforgettable sermons, that "the Church is no mere academic society for the satisfying of all the *quidnuncs* of an interminable contrariousness of spirit," it may also be said of its liturgical work that it is neither a museum for the pious preservation of the past nor an experimental laboratory for the testing of new enthusiasms.

Liturgical worship may legitimately be conducted "beneath the lofty dome of St. Peter's, under the leafy arches of one of Nature's cathedrals, in one of those ultramodern structures which have already arisen in parts of Europe or America, or in some future masterpiece of Indian or Chinese art." [6] Not everyone may feel equally at ease in all such, or countless other possible places; but he who prefers the simple lines of some village sanctuary has no right to call into question the superior appeal, for other tastes, of the Baroque splendors of the Abbey Church at Melk or of the Chiesa di Gesù at Rome.[7] The underlying point of unity is neither aesthetic nor material; it is rather doctrinal.

Differing types and kinds of architecture, of music, of liturgical observance and ceremonial have sprung up, flowered, and either decayed or endured at varying periods in Christianity's history; and it is not to be expected that our own time, which has tellingly been called *the age of the least common denominator,* would fail to yield to the compulsion of making its own contribution. The seemingly sudden eruption of many extreme expressions of the spirit of contemporaneity has given rise to quite understandable tensions. These work rather toward obfuscation than toward clarification in the discussion of such matters today, and make very difficult any attempt to evaluate certain present-day movements in religious life and to accord to them a just place in the whole context of Christian worship. But what is most important to remember is that, as God the Father surveyed His creation and found it good, man must be mindful of his own nature and fulfill his proper function by searching and proving what he himself has wrought. The creative urge which God has given to man, and which mirrors the vast activity of the Divine Hand, is not one, alas, before whose every result we can stand in the same kind of awe as is spontaneously evoked by the work of its Great Prototype. Man's work, unlike God's, proceeds on the system of trial and error.

If we seek an underlying bond of reality and unification, we are likely to find it, I think, not so much in an aesthetic or in a material consideration, but, as has been said, in a doctrinal one. It is, therefore, to be recognized that a driving impulse, born of grace, has ever spurred the Christian Church to carry out the Master's mandate that all things whatsoever He had commanded be proclaimed and taught throughout the world. Man's deep-seated realization of his own response to a divine command is nowhere so strikingly or so perduringly exemplified as in the characteristic concern for liturgical action which has moved

saints and scholars from the earliest ages down to the Fathers of the Second Vatican Council in their solicitude to promote fuller participation in the Mass, the supreme act of Catholic worship. For, indeed, as has been well said, "it is the Mass that matters"; it is the Mass—and their adherence to it—that best expresses, insofar as Catholics are concerned, the characteristic stamp of their manner of worship, of their whole philosophy of religion that differentiates them from others. A learned ecclesiologist of the past generation paid tribute to a certain great religious fraternity that exercised a prominent role in the formation of the *ethos* distinctive of post-Reformation Catholicism by saying that it was by them that "Europe was taught to hold hard by the doctrine of the Mass."[8] This teaching the European missioners transplanted to America, thus marking American Catholicism with the same essential note of devotion to the great Eucharistic Act. So it is that, even in an age like our own, remarkable for ecumenicity of spirit and an irenic desire to recognize and to embrace whatever is good among the usages and beliefs of those who differ from us, this still remains true. It could not be otherwise without a relinquishment of our heritage.

A modern Roman theologian has summed up the reason for this by declaring:

In harmony with universal belief, Catholic faith maintains that the supreme act of worship is the sacrificial act, but it also adds to this belief the statement that when the sacrificial act had ceased to be merely symbolic and, after Christ had fulfilled figures in reality, then the rite of sacrifice acquired a new, unique, and wholly complete value because it embodied the reality it expressed. Just as all the acts of worship ordered by Moses were focussed on sacrifice, so also all elements of religion, elevated to the height of their perfection, are made one in the Mass. The old oblation has not passed away, for the first fruits and symbols of life are still offered in the bread and the wine; but in the more spiritualized Christian worship these realities are no more than a mystical veil by means of which the Word of God gives Himself to man as the *bread of life* and the *draught of immortality.*

The immolation is still made, but, the reign of darkness being fled, it is the Christ Himself Who is the victim. The flesh and the blood of the Man-God are represented under different symbols, symbols which become *mortis indices*

168

in remembrance of His Passion while at the very same time, as bread and wine, they are given the sense of symbols of life, a life which takes its root in His death. The elements of the offering as well as those of the unbloody death are symbols of the Creation and emblems of the Redemption: they are re-united and identified in the sacrifice of the Mass; for the Redemption is Creation restored.

By means of these first fruits of creation, which are transformed into the body and blood of Jesus, the Church receives from God Himself the gifts of offering; and by a divine change these gifts become seeds of life sown in the furrows of time to the end that they may blossom everlastingly.[9]

No one can deny that so stupendous a mystery as the Eucharist is difficult of comprehension. No one can avoid recognizing that the even partially understood devotion of countless generations of Catholics to the Mass has resulted in their possessing a source of renewal in individual and in corporate spiritual life which gives their religion a value unique in history. No one at all cognizant of human nature, of man as a creature wondrously compounded, being *part mortal clay and part ethereal fire*,[10] doubts that man needs further instruction, constant reaffirmation, and continuing restatement of so sublime a reality if it is to become a fecund principle in his own regeneration and in his effort to re-form the world to the Image of Christ. During their recent deliberations, the Fathers of the Second Vatican Council devoted much time and thought to the solution of this and cognate problems as they are typified in the spectacle of modern man confronted with, and not understanding, the Great Eucharist, the Mass. And, in their pastoral desire to awaken Christians of our own time to the outpouring of creative love and redeeming force which the Mass bespeaks, they have determined to make certain changes in the manner of its celebration. These changes have been initiated by the Council's Constitution on the Sacred Liturgy. The essential and abiding note of the Mass remains unchanged, the very embodiment of the work wrought by Christ—mankind's Redemption.

It is not to be expected that the task of revising the manner in which the central act of Catholic worship is performed can be undertaken with entire success or with complete satisfaction to everyone who has an interest in it. There are always to be considered old customs that memory lovingly recalls and loyalty reluctantly abandons; and not everyone is inclined to choose the self-same solution to difficulties and anomalies irritating to some and quite unperceived by others. The basic purpose of the reform is to make attendance at divine worship, regarded by Catholics as a compulsory obligation, a matter of greater urgency to individual worshipers. Whether what some consider the unique means of attaining this laudable end are the only or the best ones which might be encouraged is something only the future will establish. Juridically, the decision in these matters is in the hands of the local bishops; for the Council and the Roman authorities have inaugurated permissive rather than mandatory changes.

It is the bishops alone who have an obligation, *in conscience,* to deal with the practical aspects of the matter; and there seems reason for believing that, where some of the permissions to change old usages for new ones have not been availed of, this may be due to a conviction on the part of the Ordinaries that such means are not called for within their jurisdictions. The whole matter is still admittedly within the experimental stage; and this prohibits an apodictic solution of the many problems posed by certain issues of the day.

AUTHOR'S PREFACE

[1] Cf. Auguste Croegaert: *The Mass: A Liturgical Commentary,* abridged Eng. trans. of *Les Rites et les Prières du saint Sacrifice de la Messe* (Malines: H. Dessain) by J. Holland Smith (London: Burns & Oates, 1959) Vol. I, pp. 78–82; Vol. II, pp. 1–8, 133–139; J. Lebreton: *Histoire du Dogme de la Trinité* (Paris: Beauchesne, 1928) Vol. II, 177–81. See also Bernard Capelle: *A New Light on the Mass,* trans. by a monk of Glenstal from the conferences, *Pour une meilleure intelligence de la Messe* (Dublin: Clonmore and Reynolds, Ltd., 1952) pp. 9–10; Bickell: *Messe und Pascha* (Mainz, 1872) trans. and ed. by Skene as *The Lord's Supper and Paschal Ritual* (Edinburgh, 1891); W. O. E. Oesterley: *Jewish Background of the Christian Liturgy* (Oxford: Clarendon Press, 1925); F. S. B. Gavin: *The Jewish Antecedents of the Christian Sacraments* (London: S. P. C. K., 1928); Felix L. Cirlot: *The Early Eucharist* (London: S. P. C. K., 1939); Gregory Dix: *The Shape of the Liturgy* (Westminster: Dacre Press, 1954) esp. pp. 48ff; Antonio Piolanti: *The Holy Eucha-*

rist; Eng. trans. by L. Penzo (New York: Desclée, 1961) pp. 17ff and bibliography pp. 31ff; Benedict Steuart: *The Development of Christian Worship* (London: Longmans, Green, and Co., 1953) pp. 3–9. It is notable that not one of the psalms used at the Jewish festival appears in any form in the oldest part of the Mass, the Canon. Dom Leclercq points out that the psalms and prayers said at the Pasch were replaced in the Mass by prayers inspired by them. Most of the early Christians came from Judaism; they had to be told that the Old Law had come to an end and had made way for the New. If the former character of the Pasch had been preserved by relating its ceremonies and prayers openly to the Last Supper, these new converts might have lost sight of the true meaning of the Christian Eucharist. Many writings of the period, such as the Epistle to the Hebrews and the Epistle attributed to St. Barnabas, bear the mark of a necessary reaction against Jewish rites. Cf. Henri Leclerq: "Messe" in *Dictionnaire d'Archéologie Chrétienne et de Liturgie,* 11, 531–532.

[2] St. Thomas Aquinas: *Sacris solemniis,* hymn assigned to Matins of Corpus Christi in the *Breviarium Romanum,* and for the Procession at Mass on that day in the *Graduale Romanum.* The text, with a prose translation, may be seen in Joseph Connelly: *Hymns of the Roman Liturgy* (Westminster, Maryland: Newman Press, 1958) pp. 120–123. Note also how Aquinas plays upon the same idea in his Sequence for the Mass of Corpus Christi, *Lauda Sion Salvatorem* (text in Connelly: *op. cit.,* pp. 124–127), especially in the verses: *In hac mensa novi regis,* / *Novum Pascha novae legis* / *Phase vetus terminat.* / *Vetustatem novitas,* / *Umbram fugat veritas* / *Noctem lux eliminat.* (In the translation of the late Msgr. Hugh T. Henry: At the new King's sacred table, / The new law's new pasch is able / To succeed the ancient rite: / Old to new its place hath given, / Truth has far the shadows driven, / Darkness flees before the Light.—H. T. Henry; *Eucharistia* (Philadelphia: Dolphin Press, 1912) p. 39.)

[3] See the description in Sir John Stainer: *The Music of the Bible,* rev. and ed. by F. W. Galpin (London: Stainer & Bell, 1907).

[4] "We can but admire," says the late Fr. Ellard, S.J., in his study of Alcuin, "the careful, conscientious, and humane fashion in which Alcuin's allotted task was completed." (G. Ellard: *Master*

Alcuin, Liturgist: a Partner of our Piety [Chicago: Loyola University Press, 1956] p. 127.)

[5] For a detailed consideration of a particular instance of this kind of liturgical enrichment, see Alastair Guinan: "Our Lady as Intercessor for the Departed: A Glance at Liturgical Life in France under the Ancien Régime;" *Theological Studies* XV (September 1954) pp. 416–430.

[6] *Acta Apostolicae Sedis* 39 (1947).

[7] This passage, taken from Aquinas, occurs in par. 47 of the Constitution.

[8] *AAS* 48 (1956) 725.

[9] The use of the vernacular, as envisioned by the Council in greater or lesser degree throughout the Mass, is permissive and not mandatory. Cf. decree of May 1, 1964, of the Roman Commission charged with the execution of the Conciliar Constitution. Its introduction depends upon the prudent judgment of the local authority (i.e., the Ordinary of any given place) concerning its usefulness; and any amplification of existing concessions transcends even that jurisdiction; all such cases must be separately submitted to the decision of the Holy See. (Cf. pars. 36 and 40 of the Constitution on the Liturgy and pars. 57 and 58 of the decree of September 26, 1964.) The Council, moreover, distinctly provides (par. 36 of the Constitution) that "the use of the Latin language is to be preserved in the Latin rites," and (par. 54) that steps be taken that congregations may be able "to say or sing together in Latin . . . the Ordinary of the Mass . . ."

[10] Provision was made in the Missal of Trent, a book which has been in use since the time of Pius V, for this method of saying Mass; cf. *Missale Romanum ex decreto sacrosancti Concilii Tridentini restitutum, Rit. serv.* . . . . V, 3. Eighteenth-century French diocesan Missals (e.g. Paris, 1737; Lyon, 1771; and Fréjus, 1786), also make provision for the saying of Mass facing the congregation. Some "old-fashioned" Anglican clergy used to celebrate at the north end of the Communion Table with the idea of keeping the progress of the rite open to the people assisting at it. On the subject of the celebration of Mass facing the people, see the discussion of the matter in Croegaert, *op. cit.,* 1, pp. 12–15; and an important article by Père Louis

Bouyer of the French Oratory, "La Messe et Nos Églises," *La France Catholique* (November 6, 1964), where he argues that, while the use of an altar facing the people is legitimate and desirable in certain special circumstances, it is neither "primitive" in historic usage nor always practical in our own day.

[11] This is not an innovation, but an intensification of the accepted norm set by Trent, in accordance with immemorial tradition, that the sermon be, ordinarily, an explanation of the Gospel pericope appointed for the day; and the *Caeremoniale Episcoporum*, which dates from the seventeenth century, states this principle in just so many words: *"Sermo regulariter infra Missam debet esse de Evangelio currenti"* (I, 22, 2). Cf. Ch. X on "The Homily," a new insertion in the present edition of this book.

[12] Cf. Note 1, Ch. XII.

[13] Instruction of the S.C.R. of September 26, 1964; VI, No. 60; *AAS* 56 (1964).

[14] *AAS* 48 (1956), 725.

PRELUDE

[1] *"Sacerdos ne omittet ad Eucharistici Sacrificii oblationem sese piis precibus disponere, eoque expleto gratias Deo pro tanto beneficio agere."* (CJC, c. 810.) This is also the sense of the rubrics in various Missals which urge the celebrant to make use of the prayers which they provide, or of others of his own choice. Cf., e.g. *Roman Missal: Missale Romanum . . . Americae Septentrionalis . . .* (New York: Benziger, 1964); *Rit. serv.* I, 1; and, as far as concerns the thanksgiving afterward, XII, 6; and cf. *Ordo Missae* 1965, *Rit. serv.* nn. 1, 92. Many of these prayers are richly indulgenced.

[2] Cf. "The Priest Prepares to Celebrate Mass," Ch. 6 of Croegaert: *op. cit.*, I, pp. 47–51.

[3] According to the Instruction of the S.C.R. of September 26, 1964 (par. 48), and the new *Ordo Missae* (authorized by the decree of January 27, 1965), Psalm 42 has been removed from the Ordinary of the Mass; and, on occasions when another liturgical service immediately precedes the Mass, all the prayers prior to the first kissing of the altar by the celebrant are passed over (*Ordo Missae* 1965 n. 5, *Rit. serv.* n. 22). The Dominicans, in

following their own Use, have long omitted this psalm; and, in the Missal authorized for use at Lyon in 1771, the *Judica me* is not found in the *Ordinarium Missae*, being given a place between the *Veni Creator* and Psalm 83, *Quam dilecta,* in the *Praeparatio ad Missam.*

[4] Cf. *Rit. serv.* III, 6 of the Tridentine Missal. The similar provisions, in the *Codex Rubricarum* of 1961 (nn. 424–425), prefixed to the 1964 Missal have been now superseded by the Instruction of the S.C.R. dated September 26, 1964 (Ch. II; I; n. 48c) and by the *Ordo Missae* 1965, *Rit. Serv.,* n. 23.

CHAPTER I

[1] Cf. the text of an antiphon, composed by St. Thomas Aquinas for the Office of Corpus Christi: *O sacrum convivium, in quo Christus sumitur; recolitur memoria passionis ejus: mens impletur gratia: et futurae gloriae nobis pignus datur.* These words are incorporated into par. 47 of the Conciliar document on the Liturgy. Cf. *Preface*, n. 7.

CHAPTER III

[1] Annealings and lustrations are Gallican rather than Roman and, as Msgr. Duchesne long ago pointed out, up until the sixth century, the Roman Church was without a ritual for the dedication of churches: prior to its halfway mark "a church was dedicated by the simple fact that Mass had been solemnly said within it." (*Christian Worship,* p. 404). It is to the Church of Gaul, inspired by the thought of what had been done in ancient Israel (cf. the rules found in Exodus 29 and Leviticus 8) and by the practice in vogue among Oriental Christians, that we owe the magnificent ceremony which presently occupies so many pages in the *Pontificale Romanum.* The Roman usage referred to in the letter written by Pope Vigilius to Profuturus of Braga in 538 has reference to a ceremony of funerary character in which the relics of a saint are brought to a tomb prepared for them and enclosed within it; the exterior and interior of the sepulcher are anointed, and Mass is then solemnly said over the altar tomb. In the tenth century, the beautifully symbolic ceremonial of Gallican use found its way to Rome, where it enriched the poverty of the pure Roman rite. See Duchesne: *op. cit.,* pp. 399–418; Croegaert, I, 16–38. The best discussion of the altar in general in English is still Edmund Bishop's essay "On the

History of the Christian Altar," first published in *The Downside Review* of July 1905, and reprinted in his *Liturgica Historica* (Oxford: Clarendon Press, 1918) pp. 20–38. The distinguished English architect Sir J. Ninian Comper has also given us a delightfully discursive treatment of the subject, full of suggestive insights and tenaciously held personal opinions, in his short treatise *Of the Christian Altar and the Buildings Which Contain It* (London: S. P. C. K., 1950). Geoffrey Webb's *The Liturgical Altar* (Westminster, Maryland: Newman Press, 2nd ed., rev. and enlarged, 1949) is mainly an attempt to offer a practical series of notes on the design and furnishing of the altar. Ch. VII of the Vatican Council's Constitution on the Liturgy and Ch. V of the decree of S.R.C. of September 26, 1964, promulgated officially in *AAS*, have already given rise to further discussion of the form and treatment of the altar in latter-day churches. The rubrics of the 1965 *Ordo Missae* make it quite clear that the so-called old altars are by no means to be abandoned incontinently. Cf. also *Preface*, n. 10.

Among recent publications on the subject of constructing altars, in addition to the article of Abbé Louis Bouyer referred to above (n. 10 of the *Preface*), see also the English version of Ch. V of the Instruction of September 26, 1964, jointly issued by the Conciliar Commission headed by Cardinal Lercaro and the Congregation of Rites (*Liturgical Arts* 33 [February 1965]) p. 37; the *Declarations* of the Preparatory Commission on the Liturgy (translated by Professor Herbert Musurillo, S.J., in *Liturgical Arts* 33 [November 1964] pp. 9–10); Michael J. Marx, O.S.B.: "The Altar of the Lord's Supper," in *Liturgical Arts* 33 (November 1964) pp. 4–6; Ade Béthune: "The Sacred Cupboard," in *Liturgical Arts* 32 (May 1964) pp. 90–98.

CHAPTER IV

[1] This procedure, which may look unusual to those accustomed only to the Low Mass rite of the Tridentine Missal, is actually not revolutionary; for, as will be recalled by anyone who has ever assisted at a Pontifical Mass, it is on his throne (usually the chief place in the choir, but at Lyon in the center of the apse behind the high altar) that a bishop in his own diocese, solemnly officiating at Mass, sits until the time that he goes to the altar while the Offertory Anthem is being sung. In the Papal High Mass, the Pope is at his throne during the entire first part of the Mass. And, as a matter of fact, the Pope communicates at the throne as well, a usage some writers have sought to justify by analogy with the Crucifixion having taken place upon a hill—*in loco eminentiori*. A prelate of episcopal rank who is not entitled to the use of a fixed throne in the sanctuary conducts this first part of the service from a faldstool—a kind of seat with low arms and without a back, which is set on the floor below the altar steps.

[2] According to an Instruction issued by the S.C.R. on September 3, 1958, the old practice of singing as many verses of the psalm as circumstances may require, with the repetition of the antiphon after each verse or pair of verses, may be made use of; and these directions apply also to the Offertory and Communion antiphons. As a matter of fact, this procedure was already permitted by the rubrics of the *Graduale Romanum* issued at the beginning of the present century. It is not the Vulgate Psalter texts which are found in the Introïts and other parts of the *Antiphonale Missarum*: they are taken from the old *Itala* (a Latin text dating from the second or third century) as revised by St. Jerome in 383–384. This is the old *Psalterium Romanum*. Since the time of Sixtus V (d. 1590) and Clement VII (d. 1605), another version of the Psalms, called the *Psalterium Gallicanum* (made by Jerome in 387–388) has been used in the Vulgate (and also in the Breviary until the appearance, in 1945, of another version made by the Professors of the Pontifical Biblical Institute, which Pius XII sanctioned for optional use in saying the Office). At least one other new version is presently in preparation.

Perhaps the finest commentary in English on the texts used as Introïts is C. C. Clifford's *Introibo: Readings on the Entrance Versicles of the Roman Missal* (New York: Cathedral Library Association, 1907).

[3] Cf. *Ordo Missae* 1965, *Rit. serv.* n. 23.

[4] The original meditation, as printed in the first edition, has to do with the Sign of the Cross, which the celebrating priest now no longer makes at the Introït; therefore this passage, suggested by some sentences in the great Arnauld's version of St. Augustine's *Confessions*, has been substituted. (Cf. *Les Confessions de St. Augustin, traduites en François par Monsieur Arnauld d'Andilly*. (Paris: Pierre Le Petit, 1675, pp. 311ff.)

CHAPTER V

[1] The reference is to the manuscript discovered in 1884 by Gamurrini, the authorship and the provenance of which appear to have been settled by Dom Férotin (cf. *La Révue des Questions Historiques*, October, 1903) and by Dom Fernand Cabrol in his "Études sur la Peregrinatio Silviae" in the great *Dictionnaire d'Archéologie Chrétienne et de Liturgie* (Paris, Letouzey et Ané, 1907ff). The great eighteenth-century French liturgiologist Dom Claude de Vert noted that the *Kyrie* was a form of intercessory aspiration familiar to the ancient pagans: he quotes Arrian (c. A.D. 170), who puts the following words into the mouth of the Stoic Epictetus: "And now with trembling we take hold of the bird-augur, and calling upon the god, pray to him *Kyrie eleison,* help me to get out of my trouble." (Claude de Vert: *Explication . . . des cérémonies de l'Église* [Paris, 1706]; I, 94–95.) Cf. also Epictetus: *Dissertationes ab Arriano digestae,* Lib. II, Cap. 7, ed. J. Schweighäuser (Leipzig, 1799) I, 202. It is thought that during the first century and a half of Christianity the *Kyrie* was not in use; and, even in A.D. 529, the decree of the Council of Vaison (issued under the presidency of S. Césaire d'Arles, a strong Romanizer in matters liturgical), enjoining its use, suggests that it was then a fairly recent innovation. Some have ascribed its introduction at Rome to St. Gregory the Great (590–604); but see the detailed study of this formulary in Edmund Bishop: *Liturgica Historica* (Oxford: Clarendon Press, 1918) pp. 116–136. The matter is also discussed by Dom Gregory Dix, in his *The Shape of the Liturgy* (Westminster, 1954); and there are good summaries in Steuart's *The Development of Christian Worship* (London: Longmans, Green, and Co., 1953), and in Croegaert's *The Mass: A Liturgical Commentary* (London, 1958).

[2] The original text of the *Gloria* is, like that of the *Kyrie,* in Greek. It is extant in two variant forms. One is found in the *Codex Alexandrinus* of the Sacred Scriptures, while the other is part of that curious Syriac document, the so-called *Apostolic Constitutions* (VII, 47). It seems that the Alexandrine Codex has preserved the original, and that the other version is an Arianist (or, at least, an Appolinarist) recension. There are also a number of Latin versions of the *Gloria* which differ slightly from that in our present Missals; see the interesting synoptic table in Dr. F. E. Warren's edition of the old *Bangor Antiphonary,* II, pp. 76–77, (London: Henry Bradshaw Society, 1895, publication no. 10). Cf. also the summation of the history of the use of the *Gloria* in E. G. Cuthbert F. Atchley: *Ordo Romanus Primus* (London: The De La More Press, 1905) pp. 71–72. The occasion, as well as the date, of its introduction into the Mass is in dispute. Dom Dix (*op. cit.,* p. 456, n. 1) thinks that "the *Gloria* was in fact more closely connected with Easter than Christmas at Rome"; but it certainly seems more logical to think, as M. Croegaert puts it (*op. cit.,* I, p. 136), that "At Rome, the *Gloria* was introduced into the first Mass of Christmas, celebrated before dawn, before the fifth century. This was its natural place." Originally, its use was restricted to bishops, and it was not until the eleventh century that this was extended to simple priests, although they seem at an earlier date to have been allowed to make use of it on Easter Day. Berno of Reichenau (fl. c. 1048), in a work entitled *De quibusdam rebus ad missae officium spectantibus* (Cap. ii), asks indignantly why presbyters should not be allowed to use the *Gloria* every Sunday and Festival Mass, asserting that, if its use be conceded to them on Easter Day, so much the more ought they to be allowed to sing it on Christmas Day, when it was first heard. (Cf. Atchley: *op. cit.,* p. 72). Cranmer, in the Anglican Prayer Book of 1552, transferred the *Gloria* from its place before the Collects (where it stood in the Book of 1549) to a new position, after the Communion, and immediately preceding the Blessing. Dom Dix cites W. Lockton (*The Remains at Eucharist* [Cambridge, 1920; p. 184]) as suggesting that this was done under the influence of Zwingli. (Cf. Dix: *op. cit.,* pp. 667ff). The revisors of the American Prayer Book in 1928 did not change the arrangement fixed by Cranmer; but, in many Anglican churches, it is actually sung after the *Kyrie,* as in the Roman use.

CHAPTER VI

[1] If the celebrant be at the altar and already facing the people, he does not, of course, turn. (Cf. *Ordo Missae* 1965, *Rit. serv.,* n. 34). This provision was made also in the Tridentine Missal in respect to Mass said *versus populum.* (Cf. *Rit. serv.* V, 3). And the same is true of the Paris Missal of 1738, of the Lyon book of 1771, and of that of Fréjus of 1786.

[2] Formerly this prayer was marked *Secreta* in the Latin Missal. See n. 2 of Ch. XVI, *infra*.

[3] The principle of standing at the Collects was always maintained at chanted Masses, except on days of penitence or in Masses for the dead. At Low Masses, by a custom sanctioned by the *Rubricae generales* XVII, 2, of the Tridentine Missal, those in attendance were directed to kneel throughout, even in Paschal time, except for the reading of the Gospel, when they were told to stand. The omission of this paragraph in the new *Codex Rubricarum* would appear to imply that the directions given (Cap. X; nn. 517–523) for chanted Masses are to be followed at Low Mass; but the direction to kneel at the Collects in ferial Masses of Advent, Lent, and Passiontide, of the September Ember Days, at IInd and IIIrd class Vigil Masses out of Paschaltide, and in Masses for the dead, is specifically maintained (n. 521c).

[4] Should the celebrant not be at the altar for the reading (or chanting) of the Collect, he simply bows his head in whatever direction he may be facing. This new rubric (cf. *Ordo Missae* 1965, *Rit. serv.* 33) eliminates the fine distinctions formerly made in respect to such bows (see the *Rit. serv.* of the Tridentine Missal, V, 2).

[5] There has been published in the series *Études liturgiques: Collection dirigée par le Centre de Pastorale Liturgique,* a work which no one who wishes to know the origin, usage, and meaning of these prayers can afford to neglect. Cf. Dom P. Bruylants, O.S.B.: *Les Oraisons du Missel: Textes et Historie,* 2 vols. (Louvain: Centre de Documentation et d'Information Liturgiques, Abbaye du Mont-César, 1952). The literature on the collects and their literary form is extensive. The following may be consulted: C. C. Martindale: *The Prayers of the Missal, I: The Sunday Collects* (New York, 1937): J. Cochez: *La Structure rythmique des oraisons* (Louvain, 1928); M. G. Haessly: *Rhetoric in the Sunday Collects* (Saint Louis, 1938); and a number of periodical publications which are cited by Mlle. Mohrmann in Botte-Mohrmann: *L'Ordinaire de la Messe* (Paris, 1953) p. 45, n. 1.

CHAPTER VII

[1] Dom Botte reminds us that by this term the New Testament writers (e.g. Luke 16: 16, 29, 31) intended to signify the whole of the Older Testament. Cf. Bernard Botte & Christine Mohrmann: *L'Ordinaire de la Messe* (Paris: Éditions du Cerf; Louvain: Abbaye du Mont-César, 1953) p. 67, n. 5.

[2] Actually, the three lessons (the same as those found in the old *Missa Praesanctificatorum* of the Tridentine Missal) appointed to be read at the opening of the Solemn Liturgy of Good Friday, according to the *editio typica* of the *Ordo Hebdomadae Sanctae* authorized by the S.C.R. on November 16, 1965, are one from *Osee* (6: 1–6), a second from *Exodus* (12: 1–11) and the *Passion,* according to St. John (18: 1–40 and 19: 1–42), so that one might say that an even better illustration of the author's description of the more ancient readings is provided by the Mass formulary of the Saturday of the Advent Ember Days where we find a Prophetic reading (sections being provided from Isaias 35: 1–7; 40: 9–11; 45: 1–8; and from Daniel 3: 47–51), a passage from an Apostolic Letter (Paul's second Epistle to the Thessalonians, 2: 1–8), and then the Gospel pericope (Luke 3: 1–6).

[3] The Instruction of the S.C.R. of September 26, 1964, and the *Ordo Missae* of 1965 provide (respectively nn. 49, 50, 52, and n. 14; *Rit. serv,* nn. 44, 46) that the Lesson or Epistle may, if read or chanted by the celebrating priest, be declaimed from the altar, or from the ambo or pulpit, or from some other convenient place within the sanctuary. Should this part of the service be entrusted to another than the celebrant, either the ambo or some other convenient place within the sanctuary area, from which the lesson may be heard by the congregation, may be used. In Low Masses or in chanted Masses without deacon and subdeacon, the lessons and epistles as well as the chants (Gradual, Alleluiatic verse, or Tract, as the case may be) are appropriately read or chanted by a competent lector or server. Aside from the greater freedom allowed in the choice of place from which this may be done and the fact that, if the Ordinary so permit, the vernacular may be used, there is nothing really new here: it was already provided, according to the Tridentine Missal (*Rit. serv.* VI, 8), that in Masses celebrated without the assistance of deacon and subdeacon a lector or reader, vested in surplice, might chant the lesson. It has long been the custom in many French churches to entrust this duty to a chorister.

CHAPTER IX

[1] The rubrics referred to in the preceding note (Instruction, nn. 49, 50, 52; and *Ordo Missae* 1965, nn. 13, 14, 15; *Rit. serv.* nn. 38, 44–47) allow the same liberty of decision in the choice of the place from which the Gospel is read or chanted as is granted in respect to the Lesson or Epistle. However, only a man who has received at least the order of the diaconate may publicly read the Gospel. Of course, the celebrant has the option, in all cases, of reciting both the nonevangelical readings and the evangelical readings himself.

CHAPTER X

[1] Cf. Romans 10: 14, 15.

[2] Cf. Acts 20: 20, 31.

CHAPTER XI

[1] It is usual to ascribe this adoption to the instance of the Emperor Henry II who came to Rome in the days of Benedict VIII (1012–1024). Berno, abbot of Reichenau, states that, when the Emperor asked the Romans why they did not recite the Creed at Mass after the Gospel, he met the reply that inasmuch as the Church of Rome had never been tainted by heresy they had no need to recite the Creed. The Emperor, however, persisted and finally won the consent of the Pope that the Creed be sung at public Masses. Cf. E. G. C. F. Atchley: *Ordo Romanus Primus, with introduction and notes* (London: The De La More Press, 1905) p. 80, citing Berno of Reichenau: *De quibusdam rebus ad missae officium spectantibus libellus*, Cap. ii, in J. Cochlaeus: *Speculum Missae* (Venice, 1572) fol. 166. On the rôle of Charlemagne and his great liturgist, Alcuin, in the use of the Creed at Mass, see the recent work of Gerald Ellard, S.J.: *Master Alcuin, Liturgist; a partner of our piety* (Chicago: Loyola University Press, 1956) pp. 184–188.

[2] To the prescriptions of the Tridentine Missal concerning the use of the *Credo* (cf. *Rubricae generales*, XI) certain modifications were added, under Pius X in the Bull *"Divino afflatu,"* and by decrees of the Congregation of Sacred Rites (*Additiones et variationes in rubricis Missalis* VII), including the decree *"Cum nostra"* of 1955, simplifying the rubrics of Breviary and Missal. All are now superseded by the *Codex Rubricarum,* which took effect in 1961. Nn. 475 and 476 are concerned with the Creed, enjoining its use on every Sunday; on first-class feasts and in votive Masses of the first class; on second-class feasts of Our Lord and of Our Lady; during the Octaves of Christmas, Easter, and Pentecost; on the natal festivals of Apostles and Evangelists; on the feasts of St. Peter's Chair (February 22); and on that of St. Barnabas. Prior to 1956 the Creed was attached to the feast of St. Mary Magdalene (July 22), who has been thought of as being the *Apostola Apostolorum;* and some liturgists may regret this deprivation.

CHAPTER XII

[1] The Congregation of Rites and the post-Conciliar Commission have provided (cf. the Instruction of September 26, 1964, n. 56, referring to article 53 of the Constitution; and the *Ordo Missae* 1965, n. 18; *Rit. serv.,* n. 51) that, in places where the general intercession known as the Prayer of the Faithful is used, it is to be inserted into the service before the Offertory Anthem and following upon this *Oremus.* The Prayer is to be directed by the celebrant, from his seat, from the altar, from the ambo or lectern, or from the edge of the sanctuary, as he may find convenient. Should it be desired to introduce these prayers in places where they have not customarily been employed, competent territorial authority (i.e., the Ordinary) may do so. The celebrant says or intones the words of introduction; and the invocations may then be given out by a deacon, by a cantor, or by another qualified server, while the people make the litanic response. At the end, the celebrant sums up all in a collect which will ordinarily be "the prayer for any necessity" (*pro quacumque necessitate*) set forth in the Roman Missal among the *orationes ad diversa:* "O God, our refuge and strength, the very font of our devotion, be ready, we pray, to hear the Church's supplication and to grant that those things which we faithfully entreat we may in very truth obtain." But, for special reasons, other authorized collects may be used; and, of course, the rubric of the Missal set above the collect *pro quacumque necessitate* stipulates that it is not to be used on the twenty-second Sunday after Pentecost when it is the collect of the day. The Mass provided *pro quacumque necessitate* employs another collect, suitable on such an occasion.

Much has been written by liturgiologists on the history of this general intercession; cf. Duchesne:

Christian Worship, trans. by M. L. McClure, fifth edition (London: S.P.C.K., 1949) pp. 172–173; E. Bishop: *Liturgica Historica* (Oxford: Clarendon Press, 1918) p. 122.

A form of the *Great Intercession,* "Dicamus omnes . . ." generally attributed to Pope Gelasius (A.D. 492–496), is given by Dom Benedict Steuart (*op. cit.,* pp. 268–270); and two other forms, appointed for alternating use on the Sundays of Lent, according to the Ambrosian Rite as used in the Cathedral of Milan, may be found, with their proper melodies, in the *Antiphonale Missarum juxta ritum sanctae ecclesiae Mediolanensis* (Rome: Desclée, 1935); pp. 105–109, and 116–117. These latter seem entirely free of what many persons have considered to be the "offensive terminology" of the Gelasian *Deprecatio* wherein there abound such terms as *"Judaica falsitas," "heretica pravitas,"* and *"gentilium superstitio."* It is interesting to note how the Roman authorities have, in recent years, accommodated this kind of terminology to accord with the irenic fashion of the age. The Prayer for the Jews was the first to be retouched when it was progressively suggested that the word *perfidis* ought be considered as meaning not perfidious but simply *unbelieving* or *disbelieving* (1948); that it be said, like the other prayers in the series, kneeling, and be followed by the response given to them, *Amen* (1955); and finally that the word *perfidis* be entirely eliminated (1959). This last enactment of the Congregation of Sacred Rites was dramatically enforced when the late Pope John, presiding at the Good Friday service in Rome, sent his Master of Ceremonies from the Papal Throne to the altar at which the celebrating prelate had just intoned the prayer in its hitherto customary form with the order that he repeat it with the omission of the word *perfidis.* In 1965, even more thoroughgoing changes were made in the texts of four of the nine prayers presently said. As may be inferred from the statement of the Rev. Annibale Bugnini, C.M., secretary of the post-Conciliar Commission, in *L'Osservatore Romano* of March 19, 1965, the guiding principle in every case would appear to be the elimination of every phrase or suggestion which might possibly be a cause of offense to anyone, Pagan, Jew, or Christian, who is not in full external communion with the Roman Church. See the current form of these prayers. Inasmuch as this recent action of the Holy See takes generous account of the susceptibilities of non-Christians as well, it may be remarked that it goes even beyond what had been hoped for by an irenic spokesman who deprecated any phraseology offensive to "our Separated Brethren who also have the Word;" cf. M. R. O'Connell: "Gnostics on a Train," *National Review,* XVII (February 23, 1965) pp. 152–153. The same tendency is to be noted in the new titles given to votive prayers in the latest editions of the Roman Missal, where, for instance, we find a former title *contra persecutores et male agentes* replaced by *pro defensione ab hostibus,* and *contra Paganos* changed to *pro Ecclesiae libertate.* The whole is perhaps illustrative of the contemporary desire to *accentuate the positive.* Although not completely without warrant in the past (as witness the direction of the Congregation of Rites, under Leo XIII, that the prayer *contra Turcos* be excised from the Liturgy of the annual devotion to the Holy Sacrament known as the Forty Hours Prayer), this tendency is in quite striking contrast to the state of mind which prompted the issuance of the *Syllabus Errorum* under Pius IX, or even of the third paragraph of the prayer consecrating the human race to Christ the King which Pius XI ordered recited annually on that feast when he instituted it in 1925.

Independently of the question, on which liturgiologists have held varying opinions, of the precise relationship of the Good Friday Solemn Collects to the ancient *Oratio Fidelium* which some contemporary exponents of liturgical revival and reform wish to restore, it can be said that the feature of the Liturgy represented by the *Oratio Fidelium* has long been expressed by certain prayers offered, usually from the pulpit, before the sermon, and called, in France, *les prières de la Prône.* There is a valuable study of this usage in a suggestive article by James Carmody, S.J. See his "An American Use of the Prone," *Theological Studies,* 19, no. 2 (June 1958) pp. 228–236. Cf. also the form of the prone as given in *Livre d'Église Latin-François, suivant le Bréviaire et le Missel de Paris . . . Imprimé par ordre de Monseigneur l'Archevêque. Partie d'Esté* (Paris: Libraires associés . . . 1744); pp. lxiij–lxvij, where we find the Psalm *Ad te levavi* with certain versicles, and the collect, *Deus, refugium nostrum . . . ,* followed by the Psalm *De profundis, pour les morts,* with the collect, *Deus veniae largitor.*

[2] According to the new rubrics (*Ordo Missae* 1965, n. 19), the priest, who has now taken his place at the altar regardless of what option he had selected in respect to his position in the Ante-Mass

or Liturgy of the Word, does not recite the Offertory verse at a chanted Mass (when it is sung by the choir), or even at a Low Mass should it be recited by the congregation (*Rit. serv.* 1965, n. 53).

[3] This is a practice which has found general favor among many devoted to the liturgical revival; but see the objections to it (anticipated, in some places, by the suggestion that tongs be used) made in a symposium, "Comments on the 'New' Liturgy," in *Jubilee* (New York, Vol. 12, no. 11 [March 1965]), p. 17, in a letter signed "Laywoman, Carbondale, Ill." The Offertory Procession itself, in some of its variant forms, has been described by Canon Croegaert (*op. cit.*, II, pp. 74ff.)

The matter of the revival of this procession has served to spur suggestive discussion of certain theological concepts fundamental to the nature of the Mass. The Abbot of Mont-César, Louvain, who points out that "the procession does not go back to primitive times," thinks that, although when "well understood, it can be . . . a very efficacious way of reminding the faithful soul that it is he who is offering the sacrifice by the ministry of the priest"; it is also, as he puts it, very often "taken in the wrong sense" and may then "be gravely prejudicial to the true understanding of the Mass." (Cf. Bernard Capelle: *A New Light on the Mass* (Dublin: Clonmore & Reynolds, Ltd., 1952) pp. 25, 52–53, n.). The point at issue is closely tied in with the essential note of the Roman Mass, seen as being the Sacrifice of Christ, and with the concept of the oneness of the bread which is broken so that all may feed upon it (I Cor. 10:17); and Dom Capelle and other theologians seem rightly to fear the disposition exhibited by some enthusiasts to see the large host of the celebrating priest as being the symbol of Christ even as they regard the smaller hosts which they offer as being the symbol of the faithful. From the theological viewpoint which best represents the faith of the Latin Church there are, as Dom Capelle says, "not many hosts, but one, one simple bread, as at the Last Supper, and *it is offered by all.* This bread is Christ, it is not ourselves and our life." (*Loc. cit.*)

From this point there open, for the thoughtful student of the Roman Mass, certain interesting aspects of theological speculation upon which not all commentators are in agreement at the present time. An area of contrast is very readily seen to exist between the doctrine to which Dom Capelle here alludes and some other views of the Eucharist.

Continental and, nowadays, American Catholic writers are displaying a lively concern with the matter; and, among Anglicans, it has long been a subject of more or less intensive discussion. The Victorian theologian Dean Stanley has a suggestive passage in his study of Westminster Abbey wherein he notes that the term *altar* "is nowhere applied to the Holy Table in the Liturgy or Articles. But it is used of the Table of Westminster Abbey in the Coronation Service issued by order of the Privy Council at the beginning of each reign. It is there preserved with other antique traditions which have disappeared everywhere else." (A. P. Stanley: *Memorials of Westminster Abbey* (New York: A. D. F. Randolph & Co., 1887) Vol. III, p. 237, n.). He goes on to develop the idea that nowhere else "could the word be so consistently applied with the tenor of the Reformed Liturgy," inasmuch as the only acceptable sacrifice it knows is *that of praise and thanksgiving, of human lives and hearts.* He thus draws a direct contrast between this use of the word *altar* and that long associated in Catholic thought in connection with the Sacrifice of the Mass. Other Church of England men, particularly those of the Anglo-Catholic school of thought, have held other notions; but the theological bent exemplified by Dean Stanley continues to have its advocates. Edward Arbuthnott Knox (father of the late Monsignor Ronald Knox), who was long Bishop of Manchester, wrote a book called *Sacrament or Sacrifice* (London, 1914), specifically to demonstrate the distinction between what he himself calls "the 'Catholic' doctrine of the offering of a Sacrifice with the Protestant doctrine of a feast upon a Sacrifice once for all offered." (That he is not today forgotten in his desire to repudiate the first of these as being "wholly alien teaching" is sufficiently indicated by remarks of the present Rector of Grace Church, New York, the Reverend Dr. Benjamin Minifie, in *The Witness*, 50 (April 1, 1965) no. 12, pp. 8–10, wherein he refers to the Eucharist as a Sacrifice, but "not in the Roman sense"). Dr. Knox prided himself upon being among the most influential opponents of the Revised Prayer Book, advocated by many Anglo-Catholics and rejected by Parliament in 1927. (Cf. E. A. Knox: *Reminiscences of an Octogenarian, 1847–1934* [London: Hutchinson & Co., 1934] p. 323.) And Dean Inge, with his usual perspicacity, has pointed up the connection in which this was so by telling us that had the bishops who supported the Book "declared at the beginning that they would not sanction any changes in the service for Holy Communion after the prayers for the Church militant, this would have secured the passage of the Revised Book." (W. R. Inge: *Diary of a Dean* [New York: The Macmillan Company, 1950] p. 125.) There is a fairly full discussion of the Anglican theological background in Eucharistic theology in the report of the Commission on Christian Doctrine appointed by the Archbishops of Canterbury and York in 1922, which was published in 1938 under the title *Doctrine in the Church of England* (New York: The Macmillan Company) esp. pp. 139–186. Pointed reference is made here to this kind of theorizing about the Eucharist because of the growing tendency among many Catholic writers of the day to stress the Mass as being rather *Banquet* than *Sacrifice*. That it is a Banquet is true, indeed evident: St. Thomas Aquinas in his antiphon for the feast of the Holy Sacrament writes of the Eucharist as *Sacrum Convivium;* and the term is used, with great propriety, in many Catholic contexts. However, it cannot be doubted that, when used carelessly, such terminology can lead to doctrinal confusion, easily issuing in receptionism, especially in connection with some notions disproportionately exalting the priesthood of all believers. These overthrow not only the theologically acceptable idea which underlies that phrase (based, as it is, on an Apostolic use of the term "royal priesthood"), but also can lead to a misrepresentation of the Mass, which is, essentially, Christ's Sacrifice. The late Pius XII was concerned with this matter when, in speaking to the participants of the Assisi International Conference on Pastoral Liturgy in 1956, he reiterated what he had said earlier in an Allocution of November 2, 1954 (*AAS* 46 [1954] 668): "It is the priest-celebrant, and he alone, who, invested in the person of Christ, sacrifices: not the congregation, even though there be present clerics or priests reverently assisting. All these, nevertheless, can and should take an active part in the sacrifice." See also François Amiot: *Histoire de la Messe* (Paris: Arthème Fayard, 1956) pp. 67–68.

CHAPTER XIII

[1] Cf. also the formulary, at this point in the rite according to the eighteenth-century Missal of Lyon, wherein reference is made to this: "*De latere Domini nostri Jesu Christi exivit sanguis, et aqua pariter pro redemptione mundi tempore pas-*

sionis in remissione peccatorum." (*Missale sanctae Lugdunensis ecclesiae, primae Galliarum Sedis* [Lyon: A. de la Roche, 1771] p. 349). This Missal (p. 348), as well as that of Fréjus (Paris: C. Simon, 1786) p. 292, and that of Paris (Paris: A. Le Clere & Cie., 1830) p. 399, also includes, just previously to this, provision for the hallowing of the *pain bénit*, and also for the ceremony of "the faithful with candles in their hands . . . going to the Offertory" described by Canon Croegaert (*op. cit.*, II, p. 78) as surviving, nowadays, at funeral Masses in some countries. "They [the offerers] kiss," Croegaert says, "the offering dish, the paten, to show that they want peacefully and lovingly to share in the priest's oblation; then they make a pecuniary 'oblation' which replaces the ancient oblation of natural products" (*loc. cit.*). Both the Fréjus and Paris books speak of the kissing of the paten, each carefully noting that the concave side is presented to those in Major Orders, the convex side to all others; but at Lyon, it was the *pax-brede*, or *instrumentum pacis*, which was offered to be kissed by all.

CHAPTER XV

[1] Dom Botte points out that in the Sacramentaries of the medieval period are found many prayers beginning "*Suscipe, Sancta Trinitas . . .*" He thinks them to be "of Gallican origin;" for, as he says, "the old Roman liturgy always directed prayer to the Father, not to the Trinity."—Dom Bernard Botte, O.S.B. and Christine Mohrmann: *L'Ordinaire de la Messe; texte critique, traduction, et études* (Paris: Les Éditions du Cerf, 1953) p. 73, n. 1. In this connection it is interesting to recall how late Rome was in admitting into her liturgical calendar a special festival in honor of the Trinity. Cf. also Croegaert: *op. cit.*, II, pp. 106ff.

[2] This interesting feature of the old Lyonnais rite was preserved in the revision that liturgy underwent in the time of Msgr. Antoine de Malvin de Montazet (archbishop of Lyon 1758–1788). Cf. *Missale sanctae Lugdunensis ecclesiae, primae Galliarum sedis* (Lyon: A. de La Roche, 1771) p. 350. This is a usage also in accord with certain old manuscripts, e.g., the ninth-century Sacramentary of Saint-Thierry, *Reims* 213 (E. 320) [Martène: *De antiquis Ecclesiae ritibus*, I, c. 4, art. 12 Ordo IX], and the eleventh-century Sacramentary of Saint-Denis, *Paris, Bibl. Nat. lat.* 9436 [Martène:

loc. cit. Ordo V]; cf. B. Botte & C. Mohrmann: *L'Ordinaire de la Messe* (Paris: Les Éditions du Cerf, 1953) p. 72, n. c.

CHAPTER XVI

[1] Cf. Croegaert: *op. cit.*, II, pp. 123–124. The Dominican rite has the bidding *Orate fratres . . .*, but does not employ the response: the same peculiarity distinguished the old Roman Mass of the Presanctified now replaced by the service in the Holy Week *Ordo* authorized for use beginning in 1956. Formerly, only the first two words of the bidding prayer, *Orate fratres,* were said aloud by the priest, who continued the formulary quietly while the minister responded, *Suscipiat . . .* (cf. the *Rit. serv.* of the Missal, VII, 7); but the new *Ordo Missae* of 1965 directs (n. 29) that the entire bidding be said *voce congrua,* which means that, in Low Masses at least, the whole of it will be audible. The server will then reply, *Suscipiat . . .* The priest is no longer to add *Amen* to this response. Over the centuries there have been many variants in this formulary, which appears to be of Gallican origin.

[2] Cf. Ch. VI, *supra.*

[3] The Latin word *secernere,* of which *secreta* is the past participle, means *to separate, to set apart from.* Cf. the interesting account of variant explanations, with bibliographical references, given in Croegaert: *op. cit.*, II, pp. 125–129.

CHAPTER XVII

[1] There has been much discussion among scholars concerning the most just translation and the exact significance of the word *Praefatio.* Cf. the interesting and suggestive summary of opposed (and, at times, complementary) views of the matter which is given by Dom Benedict Steuart in his recent book, *The Development of Christian Worship: an outline of liturgical history* (London: Longmans, Green and Co., 1953) esp. pp. 92–96. There is a very full discussion of the preface in Croegaert: *op. cit.*, II, pp. 130–175, wherein almost every aspect of the subject is covered or suggested.

[2] That these improvisations were at times more spontaneous than judicious is sufficiently indicated by Msgr. Duchesne (cf. his *Christian Worship,* trans. by M. L. McClure; fifth edition [London: Society for Promoting Christian Knowledge, 1949] pp. 141–143); and we may well be thankful, for the decorum of our worship, that we nowadays have a book in which what is to be declaimed is set down beforehand.

[3] When, in 1738, the archbishop of Paris, Msgr. de Vintimille du Luc, issued his magnificent revision of the Missal, he wisely justified the increased number of Prefaces which marked it by the observation that he thus recalled an earlier day in the Roman liturgy when "almost every Mass had its own proper Preface." Cf. *Missale Parisiense . . . D. Caroli-Gaspar-Guillelmi de Vintimille Parisiensis Archiepiscopi auctoritate . . . editum . . .* (Paris: A. Le Clere & Cie., 1830) mandatum, p. vi. This Missal has nineteen prefaces; the Lyon Missal of 1771 has twenty-one; the Fréjus Missal of 1786 is especially rich, with thirty-eight. Among these are not only prefaces for Advent, the Blessed Sacrament, All Saints, and Dedication festivals (all of which have, in our own time, been again authorized by Rome for use *aliquibus in locis;* cf., e.g., the appended prefaces in the Missal published for the dioceses of the United States in New York in 1964), but also many others, such as that of St. John the Baptist of which Canon Croegaert (cf. *op. cit.*, II, p. 170) and others have expressed the wish that it might come again into general use. For the text of the beautiful preface *de B. Mariae pro defunctis,* found in the Fréjus Missal of 1786, and a discussion of its high theological significance, see Alastair Guinan: "Our Lady as Intercessor for the Departed: A Glance at Liturgical Life in France under the Ancien Régime," *Theological Studies* XV (September 1954) pp. 416–430.

CHAPTER XVIII

[1] The *Ordo Missae* 1965 dispenses with the bow formerly made by the celebrant while saying the *Sanctus,* and also with the sign of the Cross at *Benedictus qui venit.* Nor is anything any longer said of the ringing of the little bell (*campanulum;* cf. the *Rit. serv.* VII, 8, of the Missal formerly in use). A modern Italian commentator explicitly states even in regard to Mass being celebrated privately: "*Non si suona il campanello.*" (Carlo Braga, C.M.: *Le Ceremonie della Messa secondo l'Ordo Missae rinnovato;* Bibliotheca Ephemerides

Liturgicae; Sectio Practica, 15 [Rome: Edizione Liturgiche, 1965] p. 28.) The English liturgist Adrian Fortescue had long ago suggested that at High Mass the ringing of the bell was not a necessity, the ceremonies and the singing making the whole point sufficiently obvious; but, in a decree dated October 25, 1922, the Congregation of Rites had given four reasons for declaring it obligatory even in chanted Masses. The new rubrics seem to have now settled the question in Fortescue's favor. They also appear to suggest that *Te igitur* is not begun before the completion of the dual formulary, a requirement that seems likely to cause difficulty to choirmasters. However, Braga remarks that the celebrant is to begin *Te igitur* after the *Sanctus*, unless it be prolonged (" . . . *dopo il canto del Sanctus, a meno che non si potragga a lungo.*"—Braga: *op. cit.*, p. 57).

[2] However, cf. Edmund Bishop: *Liturgica Historica* (Oxford: Clarendon Press, 1918) pp. 131–132. Croegaert sums up much modern research on the history of the *Sanctus* (*op. cit.*, II, pp. 177–179).

[3] This word has a long history in the Old Testament. Very many translations of the Missal render the expression *Deus Sabaoth* (which is the Hebrew *Jahvé Saba'ot*) as "God of hosts." The general French usage has been "Dieu des armées" (cf. *Livre d'Église Latin-François . . . Imprimé par ordre de Monseigneur l'Archevêque* [Paris: P. G. Le Mercier, 1744] p. lxxv; and *Petit Paroissien . . . de Poitiers* [Poitiers: F.-A. Barbier, 1843] p. 187); but in the new translation of the Mass Ordinary prepared at the instance of the *Centre de Pastorale liturgique* at Paris, the rendering is "Dieu des Forces célestes." D. Botte remarks that, although it would seem that in the liturgy of the Mass the "hosts" are chiefly those of angels, the word nevertheless does retain a cosmic significance. Cf. Bernard Botte & Christine Mohrmann: *L'Ordinaire de la Messe* (Paris: *op. cit.*, p. 81, n. 1). There is a thorough discussion of the nature and history of the Canon and its text, containing much valuable information, in the work of Canon Croegaert so frequently referred to; cf. Vol. 2, pp. 184ff; and see also Capelle: *op. cit.*, pp. 37–46.

[4] See the discussion of *Benedictus qui venit* in E. G. Cuthbert F. Atchley: *Ordo Romanus Primus* (London: Alexander Moring, Ltd, The De La More Press, 1905) pp. 94–95.

CHAPTER XIX

[1] The exact force of this word in this place is much debated among latter-day liturgiologists (see the summary of opinions advanced in Dom Benedict Steuart's study, *The Development of Christian Worship* [London: Longmans, Green, and Co., 1953] esp. pp. 101–105); and D. Botte goes so far as to declare forthrightly that in fourth-century Latin *igitur* is no stronger than the Greek postpositive conjunction δε (Cf. Botte: *op. cit.*, p. 75, n. 9), which, as the grammarians commonly tell us, is very often to be entirely omitted in translation; and this is the course which D. Botte has followed in his new French version of the Ordinary of the Mass.

CHAPTER XX

[1] See, however, note 1, Chapter xxix (p. 154), where this point is more fully discussed.

[2] Moreover, as Dom Botte justly says, "in all liturgies, the recitation of the institution of the Eucharist rests upon a tradition which is independent of the evangelical accounts . . . [but] an effort has been made to blend the two factors into a symmetrical unit, and to find an expression of them which is close to the Gospel text." Cf. Botte: *op. cit.*, p. 81, n. 1.

[3] Cf. "This expression is borrowed from St. Paul and is to be taken in the Pauline sense: the Eucharist is *the* mystery of the faith, that is to say, it contains and reveals the whole economy of redemption." B. Botte: *op. cit.*, p. 81, n. 3.

[4] Perhaps attention may usefully be called here to the very illuminating paper by Professor Arthur Darby Nock of Harvard in *Mnemosyne*, 1952, on the very wide sense in which the term *sacramentum* (which is the Latin equivalent of the Greek *mysterion*) was used in the fourth century, and to a recent work by H. Rondet, M. Le Landais, A. Lauras, and Ch. Couturier—I refer to their *Études Augustiniennes* (Paris: Aubier, 1953)—wherein is attempted a detailed examination of the meaning of the words *sacramentum* and *mysterium* in the writings of St. Augustine. These terms are found used in that holy Doctor's writings no less than 2279 times, and M. Couturier has classified them according to rite, symbol, or mystery, and has tried to point out their underlying conformity.

⁵ The allusion which M. Daniel-Rops makes here is to the candle which, according to the old rubrics of the Missal (*M.R.: Rit. serv.* viii; 6, and *Rubricae generales xx, ad fin.*), is to be lit on the Epistle side of the altar by the server at this point in the Mass and is not to be extinguished until after the Communion. The new *Codex rubricarum* of 1961, n. 530, commends this custom and stipulates that where it exists it is to be kept; but it is to be remarked that some who formerly maintained it are now progressively abandoning it. The date of the introduction of this candle is uncertain; and, although latterly it was its mystic significance that seemed most important, it may originally have had some practical object as being either a means of added light for the celebrant or an imitation of the use of torches at sung Masses.

CHAPTER XXI

¹ We here touch upon the fascinating question of the *essential nature* of sacrifice and how it is effected, a point which has exercised the attention of theological writers for centuries; cf. the remarks made by D. Benedict Steuart in the introduction to his book already cited; pp. xx-xxiii. The whole question has been suggestively treated in our own day by Père M. de la Taille in his *Mysterium Fidei* (Paris: Beauchesne, 1921; Eng. trans. [by Carroll and Dalton] *The Mystery of Faith* 2 vols., New York: Sheed & Ward, 1940-50), and by M. l'Abbé Lepin in his *L'idée du sacrifice de la messe d'après les théologiens* (Paris, 1926). Cf. also the article of A. Michel "La Messe chez les théologiens postérieurs au Concile de Trente" in Vacant-Mangenot: *Dictionnaire de Théologie Catholique* (Paris, 1928) X (1); cc. 1143-1316. A particularly useful summary exposition of varying views held, within the Church, upon this question will be found in Edward F. Dowd: *A Conspectus of Modern Catholic Thought on the Essence of the Eucharistic Sacrifice* (Washington, D.C.: The Catholic University of America, 1937).

CHAPTER XXII

¹ In some manuscript Sacramentaries (as, for example, in that known as the Sacramentary of Saint-Thierry, in the Library at Reims, 213 [E. 320] [cf. Martène: *De antiquis Ecclesiae ritibus*, I, c.4, art. 12, Ordo IX], and in that which is in the Bibliothèque Nationale at Paris under the classification Ms. lat. 9428, both of which date from the ninth century), mention is here made of the Nativity as well. Cf. Botte: *op. cit.*, p. 80, n. 1.

² As, for example, at Lyon, and among the Dominicans, the Carthusians, and the Carmelites. Cf. W. R. Bonniwell: *A History of the Dominican Liturgy* (New York: J. F. Wagner, 1944) pp. 127, 186; Archdale A. King: *Liturgies of the Religious Orders* (Milwaukee, Wisconsin: The Bruce Publishing Co., 1955) pp. 51, 311, 386.

CHAPTER XXIII

¹ On both these commemorations consult the fine study of V. L. Kennedy, C.S.B.: *The Saints of the Canon of the Mass* (Rome: Pontificio Istituto di Archaeologia Cristiana, 1938). See also V. Maurice: "Les Saints du canon de la Messe au moyen âge"; *Ephemerides Liturgicae,* lii (1938) pp. 353ff.

CHAPTER XXIV

¹ The reference, in respect to the liturgy as at present constituted (according to the Decree of the S. C. R. of November 16, 1955) is to the *Missa Chrismalis* now directed to be celebrated in Cathedral Churches early on the morning of Maundy Thursday. As far as the "good things" referred to in this great Doxology in the Mass are concerned, cf. *Genesis* I. The question of the precise significance of the terms of this prayer is one which has long agitated liturgiologists, and Msgr. Duchesne has, in his usual masterly fashion, summed up the reasons for believing that these words, *Per quem haec omnia . . . bona, etc.,* indicate the presence here, at one time, of a formulary of benediction of first fruits (see L. M. O. Duchesne: *Christian Worship,* trans. by M. L. McClure; 5th edition [London: S. P. C. K., 1949] pp. 182-183); but not everyone has been satisfied with this explanation, and some recent writers have even attempted to justify the employment of this strange terminology as *originally* having pertained to the Sacred Elements themselves, (cf. the discussion of late theorizing on this head which is summed up by Dom Benedict Steuart in his *The Development of Christian Worship* [London: Longmans, Green & Co., 1953] esp. pp. 159-162, 185). Prominent among such exponents is Msgr. Callewaert who, in his "La Finale du Canon de la Messe," *Revue d'Histoire ecclésiastique,* 39 (1943) pp. 5-21, explains the reasons for his conclusions. Dom Botte evidently

thinks the question insoluble at present, for he remarks that it is not easy to see whether the words *haec omnia* apply to the objects sometimes blessed at this point in the service or only to the consecrated species. Cf. B. Botte: *op. cit.;* p. 85, n. 7. Cf. also Atchley: *op. cit.;* pp. 97–98, and 175–176; and S. J. P. van Dijk and J. Hazelden Walker: *The Origins of the Modern Roman Liturgy* (London: Darton, Longman, & Todd, 1960) pp. 307, 526–527. The Lyon Missal, authorized in 1771 by Msgr. Malvin de Montazet, makes provision at the Solemn Mass of the Transfiguration on August 6 (at which St. Xystus is commemorated) for the blessing of grapes (something which is also encountered in the old Gregorian Sacramentary) at this place. The Lyon rubric requires that, after the blessing, the grapes be removed from the altar and distributed to the attendants in the choir stalls. (Cf. *Missale Lugdunense* [1771] p. 582.) It would, perhaps, be very difficult to determine what, if any, connection exists between such customs and other curious survivals: I am thinking particularly of the distribution of nuts and raisins which used to be made during Chapel Service at Eton College in England on certain occasions. (Cf. C. Kegan Paul, Trench, Trübner, & Co., Ltd., 1899) p. 79; and Eric Parker: *Floreat* (London: Nisbet & Co., 1923) p. 62, citing W. H. Tucker: *Eton of Old.*

[2] It has for long been usual, in many places, to draw attention to this elevation by the ringing of the acolyte's bell; but this French custom was not everywhere always observed; and where Roman rubrics were rigidly adhered to and where there flourished that school of liturgists who are wont to reproach the French Church for "a fondness for overmuch bell-ringing," the Little Elevation passed in silence. Neither the present rubrics (*Ordo Missae* 1965) nor those of the Tridentine recension of what Edmond Bishop calls "the Pian or Common Rite" make any mention of a bell here (cf. the *Rit. serv.* formerly in force, IX, 3); but in the Paris Missal of 1738 we find it expressly stated: *cujus elevationis signum datur pulsatione campanulae.* Cf. *Missale Parisiense . . . D. Caroli-Gaspar-Guillelmi de Vintimille Par. Arch. auctoritate . . . editum 1738 necnon . . . D. Hyacinthi-Ludovici de Quélen, Par. Arch. jussu recognitum ac typis denuo mandatum* (Paris: A. Le Clere & Cie., 1830) p. 49, *de ritibus in Missa servandis,* Cap. II, 67.

[3] The rubrics of 1965 have introduced changes in the ceremonial here: the five signs of the Cross

formerly made, with the Host over the Chalice, are now omitted, and the whole formulary is sung or said *clara voce* while the Sacred Elements are held *slightly aloft* by the priest. At the end of the formulary, *Per ipsum . . . ,* and, after the minister or congregation has made the response, *Amen,* the celebrant places Host and Chalice again upon the altar and proceeds with the introduction to the Lord's Prayer. The melody to which the Doxology of the Canon is to be sung is printed in two forms: I) *Tonus simplex;* II) *Tonus solemnis,* in *Ritus servandus in concelebratione Missae . . .* (Typis Polyglottis Vaticanis, 1965) pp. 93–94.

CHAPTER XXV

[1] As early as 1958, the Congregation of Rites declared it permissible for the congregation at Low Mass to recite the *Pater* with the priest; the new rubrics extend this to sung Masses as well. According to the *Rit. serv.* (X, n. 75) of *Ordo Missae* 1965, the celebrant, after having covered the chalice with the pall, and having adored the holy Sacrament, rises and joins his hands before saying or singing *Oremus* and the introductory clauses to the *Pater.* "The Lord's Prayer follows," says the rubric, "which the people may sing or say in unison with the celebrant." The *Amen,* however, is now always omitted, and the priest sings the embolism aloud but alone. There has been much discussion about the necessity of waiting for "suitable melodies" for the vernacular version of this prayer.

Recently, two new versions to accompany the Latin text have been officially published and suggested for congregational use as being "more suitable for that purpose than the melodies composed for the use of the celebrant alone." The first of these, called *Tonus usualis,* is described as being "from the Spanish liturgy"; and the second, *Tonus alter,* as having been derived from "old recitatives." (Cf. *Ritus servandus in concelebratione Missae . . .* [Typis Polyglottis Vaticanis, 1965] pp. 94–96).

CHAPTER XXVI

[1] It is noteworthy that the prayers at meal times which are said according to monastic custom all have a pronouncedly Eucharistic flavor about them.

[2] This prayer, an embolism to, or prolongation of, the Lord's Prayer itself, is now chanted or said

aloud at every Mass (cf. *Ordo Missae* 1965, n. 47, *Rit. serv.* X, n. 76). This was apparently the ancient usage; but, until the present year, it had survived in the Roman Rite on Good Friday only. The melody has been published in *Ritus servandus in concelebratione Missae* . . . (Typis Polyglottis Vaticanis, 1965) pp. 96–98. The text of this prayer, beginning *Libera nos* . . . , is found in the Gelasian and Gregorian Sacramentaries; and, apart from the addition, here and there, of the names of local saints during the Middle Ages, it has always been invariable in Roman usage, although the Gallican and Ambrosian liturgies admitted of changing texts according to the day. The Roman rubrics, as presently in force, omit the sign of the Cross made by the priest with the paten, and the kissing of it, during the *Libera*.

[3] The reference here is to the rite of the *Sancta* which must not be confused with the rite of the *Fermentum,* although there are interesting analogies between the two. Both were designed to show the unity which underlies the Eucharistic celebration; but while the *fermentum* emphasized this in respect to place, the *Sancta* did so insofar as concerns time. It was anciently customary at Rome that, when the priests in charge of the various urban churches were unable to join with the Sovereign Pontiff in the celebration of Mass at the stational church of the day, he would send to them portions of one of the loaves consecrated by him. This, the *fermentum*, exemplified their **unity** with their bishop, a unity which was so stressed by St. Ignatius the Martyr when he wrote to the Church of Smyrna: "Let that Eucharist be esteemed valid which is either offered by the bishop or by him to whom he has given permission." (Cf. W. Jacobson, ed.: *Patrum Apostolicorum quae supersunt* [Oxford, 1863] II, p. 320, Cap. xx.) According to the rite of the *Sancta*, a fragment consecrated at a previous Mass was put into the chalice at *Pax Domini* to indicate that there was always the same Sacrifice, the same Eucharist, the same Communion; that the communicants at the Mass being said or sung were united with those at the previous celebration, and so on back through the ages. (Cf. Duchesne: *op. cit.*, Eng. trans.; 5th ed. [1949]; pp. 184–185; also E. G. C. F. Atchley, ed.: *Ordo Romanus Primus* [London: The De La More Press, 1905] pp. 106–109.) It is only in connection with the rite of the *Sancta* that there can be explained the custom (formerly set by the rubrics governing the celebration of the Solemn Mass) of

the subdeacon holding the empty paten wrapped in the humeral veil and raised aloft in reverence, from the time of the offertory until the Pater has been sung; for it appears that anciently the paten held the fragment of the Holy Sacrament destined to serve in the rite of the *Sancta*. It was D. Jean Mabillon, the great seventeenth-century liturgiologist, who elaborated this explanation in his own commentary on *Ordo Romanus primus* (cf. Migne: *Patrologia Latina*, LXXVII, 869–870), and in our own memory it has been sanctioned by the high authority of Msgr. Duchesne (cf. *op. cit.*, supra). Nevertheless, some modern liturgists have expressed considerable reservation in this matter. The Anglican Benedictine, D. Gregory Dix, is content with the consideration that the *provenance* of this rite is Gaul, and that it was introduced into the Roman rite only during the sixth century (cf. Dix: *The Shape of the Liturgy* [London: Dacre Press, 1945] p. 134); but the Abbot of Mont-César at Louvain, D. Bernard Capelle, is more strongly opposed to the bare notion of such a rite, and he seems to be of the opinion that it had no existence save *in the brain of D. Mabillon*. (Cf. B. Capelle in *La Revue Bénédictine*, LIII, pp. 17–22.) A great disadvantage of this new theorizing is that its acceptance would deprive us of any rational explanation for the seemingly excessive reverence with which the subdeacon was long required to treat a mere empty paten. Cf. the summary of this whole question by D. Benedict Steuart in his *The Development of Christian Worship* (1953) pp. 168–179.

CHAPTER XXVIII

[1] Dom Botte tells us that the word *judicium* used here often has in liturgical contexts a pejorative sense signifying a condemnatory sentence. It would thus seem to serve as an intensification of the word *condemnationem* which follows it. Cf. Botte & Mohrmann: *op. cit.*, p. 89, n. 1, where a reference is given to John 5: 24; and *ibid.*; p. 90, n.b., where we are bidden to take into account I Cor. 11: 29.

[2] The Dominicans, even today, employ but one of these prayers. Cf. A. A. King: *op. cit.*, p. 388. Fr. Ellard, S.J., has recently summed up the evidence, set forth by D. André Wilmart, which justifies the ascription of these two beautiful prayers to Alcuin. Cf. Gerald Ellard, S.J.: *Master Alcuin, Liturgist: A Partner of Our Piety* (Chicago: Loyola University Press, 1956) pp. 171–173.

CHAPTER XXIX

[1] Dom Benedict Steuart notes that "the whole question of the agape is still very much disputed and liturgical authorities do not agree about its true character nor the method of usage." (Cf. Steuart: *op. cit.;* p. 6). Msgr. Duchesne tells us that the Eucharistic celebration at first followed an ordinary repast partaken of in common, as may be seen from St. Paul's first Epistle to the Corinthians; "but," as Duchesne remarks, "the custom allowed of the introduction of too many inconveniences to be lasting," and "the liturgical Agape disappeared, or nearly so, within less than a hundred years after the first preaching of the Gospel." (Cf. Duchesne: *op. cit.;* p. 49, n. 1.) Of Eastern institution and observance, the *Agapé* seems never to have flourished at Rome.

[2] By the terms of a decree issued on March 7, 1965, signed by Cardinal Larraona (Prefect of the Congregation of Rites), and Cardinal Lercaro (Chairman of the Committee which has been set up to carry into effect the Conciliar provision regarding the Liturgy), there has been a partial restoration to Latin Rite Christians of the Communion under both kinds. Regulations were published, together with those affecting concelebration, in *Ritus servandus in concelebratione Missae et Ritus Communionis sub utraque specie* (Typis Polyglottis Vaticanis, 1965). Although the dogmatic decrees of Trent are specifically maintained (cf. pp. 51, 52), it is now permitted, where the Ordinary allows it, that the Sacrament of the Holy Eucharist be administered *sub utraque specie* on certain specified occasions and to certain persons. These are: 1) to the newly ordained in the Mass of Ordination; 2) to the deacon and subdeacon ministering in Pontifical and Solemn Masses; 3) to Abbesses on the day of Abbatial Blessing; 4) to nuns on the day of their Consecration; 5) to newly professed religious whose vows are made during the celebration of Mass; 6) to persons being married during a Nuptial Mass; 7) to adult converts who have just been baptized preceding the Mass; 8) to adults confirmed immediately preceding the Mass; 9) to baptized Christians on their formal reception into the Church; 10) to the persons mentioned in nn. 3–6 at the Mass of Jubilee in each case; 11) to priests and to lay brothers on the occasion of certain important celebrations. The Bishop is to select the method to be used from one of those which are explained in the rubrics (p. 51). These methods are, in respect to the Precious Blood: 1) by direct drinking from the Chalice; 2) by intinction; 3) by the use of a silver reed; 4) by the use of a spoon.

[3] The early Christians communicated standing, and during Apostolic times, as some think, even reclining. But since the latter Middle Ages, it has. been customary in the West to receive Our Lord kneeling. Perhaps the most notable attempt made, in modern times, to revive the ancient practice was that of the seventeenth-century English Puritans who (no doubt to express their disbelief in the real presence) objected very strongly to kneeling during the administration of the sacred elements. Their attitude caused the insertion into the *Book of Common Prayer* of the so-called Black Rubric, which insists on the preservation of the medieval devotional tradition of reception while "meekly kneeling." Since about the ninth century, it has been of almost universal observance in the Latin Rite that the Sacred Host be put on the tongue of each communicant, although anciently (as Tertullian, St. Cyril of Jerusalem, and St. John Damascene testify) the congregation used to accept the sacramental Bread in their right hands (the left being crossed under) and transfer It to their tongues themselves. In the tenth century, the *Ordo Romanus VI* still allowed this procedure in the case of priests and deacons.

[4] The more extended formulary, *Corpus Domini nostri Jesu Christi custodiat animam tuam in vitam aeternam,* so long familiar to us, has only lately been superseded by the present shortened form, *Corpus Christi,* which is a reversion to the usage of St. Augustine's day. In eighteenth-century France, when the longer formulary was still in use, the communicants said *Amen* in the middle of it, before the priest continued, "Custodiat . . ." (cf., e.g., *Missale Forojuliense . . . ,* 1786; *Rubricae generales* X, p. xxxvj). The custom of communicants kissing the ring of a bishop administering the Communion, before they receive the Sacred Species, is a form of the rite of the *Pax,* referred to by M. Daniel-Rops in Ch. XXVII, *supra.*

CHAPTER XXX

[1] Attractive as this idea certainly is, and spiritually suggestive as many might find it, it must be admitted that it fails to satisfy the requirements of scientific philology. Apparently, it was first proposed by Herr Dr. Kristensen in his study of

the sacrament of mission ("Het sacrament van de uitzending, missa," in *Mededelingen der Koninkl. Nederl. Academie van Wetenschappen, afd. Letterkunde,* 1949, pp. 3–15), but was shown to be based on insufficient evidence by M. l'Abbé J. Mogenet in his article "Ite missa est," in *La Revue diocésaine de Tournai,* 6 (1951); pp. 297–303. Dom Botte sums up the history of attempts to explain this formulary in the excursus upon it with which he closes his fine work on the Ordinary of the Mass. (Cf. Botte: *L'Ordinaire de la Messe* [Paris, 1953] pp. 145–149.) And more recently M. l'Abbé Amiot acidly points out that "those modern commentators who with the best of intentions suggest that *Ite missa est* means: 'Go; it is now that your own mission is beginning' are expressing an idea which is sound enough in itself but are doing so in a way calculated to cast suspicion upon their knowledge of liturgical Latin." (Cf. François Amiot: *Histoire de la Messe* [Paris: Arthème Fayard, 1956] p. 120.)

2 In medieval times bishops as well as the pope were wont to give a blessing as they left the Church in procession; and for a priest to give such a blessing at the end of the service was considered a novelty in Rome, even as late as the mid-twelfth century. So much may be gathered from the allusion to the practice made in the *Ordo* of the Lateran Basilica (Bernard of Porto: *Bernhardi cardinalis et Lateranensis ecclesiae prioris ordo officiorum ecclesiae Lateranensis,* ed. by Ludwig Fischer, in *Historische Forschungen und Quellen,* II–III (Munich and Freising, 1916) 38, no. 100). Perhaps the earliest formulary given for use during the blessing is that found in the treatise *Indutus planeta* of Haymo of Faversham, minister-general of the Franciscans (1240–1244), where the priest is told that, after the *Placeat,* he is to say: *"In unitate sancti spiritus benedicat nos pater et filius."* This formulary was shortly superseded by others, and finally by that now familiar to us. The Papal Ceremoniar, Johannes Burchard, was among the most severe critics of the older formulary; and he used it as a text in order to inveigh against *those who turned the Trinity upside down for metrical reasons.* (Cf. van Dijk and Hazelden Walker: *op. cit.,* p. 367. This book has a full discussion, with

interesting references, of the evolution of the blessing and its varied formularies.)

FOOTNOTES FOR PP. 167-169.

1 As every reader of Bishop is aware, this is a recurring theme which flows contrapuntally through all that he wrote: I am thinking, especially, of specific passages in *Liturgica Historica* (Oxford: Clarendon Press, 1918) e.g., on pp. 50, 115, 123.

2 E. P. Evans: *Animal Symbolism in Ecclesiastical Architecture* (New York: Holt, 1898) p. 308.

3 Cf. Alexandre Cingria: *La Décadence de l'Art Sacré* (Paris: À l'Art Catholique, 1930); and Louis Bouyer: *Liturgical Piety* (Notre Dame: University Press, 1955).

4 Cf. W. R. Inge: *Truth and Falsehood in Religion* (New York: E. P. Dutton, 1907).

5 J. H. Newman: *Discourses on the Scope and Nature of University Education* (Dublin: James Duffy, 1852) *Discourse IV.*

6 Alastair Guinan: "The Worship of the Whole Man," *The Month,* CLXIX (London: March 1937) p. 240.

7 See the illustrations, showing details of these and of others, in Victor-Lucien Tapié: *The Age of Grandeur: Baroque Art and Architecture,* trans. by A. Ross Williamson (New York: Grove Press, 1960).

8 Cornelius Cyprian Clifford: "Jesuitism and the Law of Prayer," *The Catholic World* 87 (April 1908) p. 42.

9 Antonio Piolanti: *The Holy Eucharist,* trans. by Luigi Penzo (New York: Desclée, 1961) p. 139.

10 Richard West: "Ad Amicos," 1. 49, in Duncan C. Tovey: *Gray and His Friends: Letters and Relics* (Cambridge University Press, 1890) p. 97.

ALASTAIR GUINAN

ABOUT THIS BOOK

AND THE MEN WHO MADE IT

HENRI DANIEL-ROPS was born Henri Jules Charles Petiot, January 19, 1901, at Epinal (Vosges), France, the grandson of peasants and the son of Colonel Charles Petiot, an artillery officer, and Odile Grosperrin. A dark-haired, slender, serious student, he majored simultaneously in law, geography and history at the University of Grenoble, winning the equivalent of a Master's degree in each subject and gaining his *agrégation* (slightly higher than a Ph.D.) from the University of Lyons before he was twenty-one. A year later he received his *habilitation*, teaching as a *professeur agrégé* at the University. He subsequently taught history at Amiens, and from 1930 until he retired from teaching in 1945, he was a professor at Neuilly. He adopted the nom de plume of Daniel-Rops for his first book—a volume of essays published in 1926— and used it for all of his prolific writings. His other books— more than seventy in all—include twenty novels, historical studies, works in the arts and sciences, poetry, and children's books. His library contained more than ten thou-

sand treasured volumes. His writings brought him many honors, including election to the Académie Française in 1955; he was the youngest member at the time. Other honors included Commander of the Order of Saint Gregory the Great in 1949 (conferred by Pope Pius XII, who was an ardent reader of his works), and the Grand Cross of that order in 1956; Commander of the Order of Christ (Portugal); Knight of the Legion of Honor; winner of the Académie Française Grand Prix de Littérature as well as its Prix Paul Flat and Prix Alfred Née. He held honorary degrees from many institutions of higher learning and he was a regular contributor to scholarly journals, as well as the editor of four series of books.

One of the most distinguished lay Catholic writers and theologians, he was the inspiration and guiding hand behind *The Twentieth Century Encyclopedia of Catholicism*. As editor-in-chief of this 150-volume series —his greatest achievement—he was proud to see it translated into nine languages, and he included in it two of his finest works, *What*

187

is the Bible? and *The Life of Our Lord.*

Daniel-Rops' intensity of feeling for the Church and her people and his painstaking research were always mirrored in his writings. His most popular and widely read book, *Jesus and His Times,* now translated into more than a dozen languages, took him three years to write. It has sold more than a half-million copies. Others of his books include: *Misted Mirror* (Knopf, 1931); *Two Men and Me* (Rockwell, 1931); *The Poor and Ourselves* (Burns, Oates & Washburne, 1938); *Israel and the Ancient World* (Longmans, 1950); *Jesus and His Times* (Dutton, 1954); *The Book of Books* and *The Book of Life* (two volumes; Kenedy, 1956); *Cathedral and Crusade* (Dutton, 1957); *This is the Mass* (Hawthorn, 1958); *What is the Bible?* (Hawthorn, 1958); *The Church in the Dark Ages* (Dutton, 1959); *The Heroes*

of God (Hawthorn, 1959); *The Miracle of Ireland* (ed.; Helicon, 1959); *The Church of the Apostles and Martyrs* (Dutton, 1960); *Golden Legend of Young Saints* (Kenedy, 1960); *Of Human Love* (Fides, 1960); *The Book of Mary* (Hawthorn, 1960); *The Protestant Reformation* (Dutton, 1961); *Monsieur Vincent* (Hawthorn, 1961); *The Catholic Reformation* (Dutton, 1962); *The Second Vatican Council* (Hawthorn, 1962); *Daily Life in the Time of Jesus* (Hawthorn, 1962); *The Church in the Seventeenth Century* (Dutton, 1963); *The Call of St. Clare* (Hawthorn, 1963); and *Bernard of Clairvaux* (Hawthorn, 1964).

In 1923 he was married to Madeleine Bouvier and they had an adopted son, Francis. Daniel-Rops died July 27, 1965, mourned by all.

FULTON JOHN SHEEN was born May 8, 1895, at El Paso, Ill., one of four sons of Newton Morris and Delia (Fulton) Sheen. He was baptized Peter and took the name of John at confirmation, later adopting his mother's maiden name. His father was a farmer, but the family later moved to Peoria, Ill., where he attended St. Mary's School and Spalding Institute, from which he was graduated in 1913. He received his B.A. and M.A. degrees from St. Viator College, Bourbonnais, Ill., where he first tasted the pleasures of speaking and writing as a member of the college debating team and newspaper staff. He completed his theological studies at St. Paul's Seminary, St. Paul, Minn., and was ordained to the priesthood for the Diocese of Peoria, September 20, 1919. A year later he obtained his degrees of Bachelor of Sacred Theology and Bachelor of Canon Law from the Catholic University of America, and went to the University of Louvain, Belgium, where he was awarded a Ph.D. in 1923. He also attended the Sorbonne in Paris

and the Collegio Angelico in Rome. In 1924 he received his Doctorate of Sacred Theology in Rome, and a year later while teaching dogmatic theology at St. Edmund's College, Ware, England, he was made an *Agrégé en Philosophie* by Louvain and awarded that university's Cardinal Mercier International Philosophy Award. His honorary degrees include LL.D., Litt.D. and L.H.D. On his return to the United States, he served as a curate of St. Patrick's Church in Peoria and joined the faculty of the Catholic University of America, Washington, D.C., in 1926 as a philosophy of religion instructor, later being promoted to a full professorship. In June, 1934, he was appointed Papal Chamberlain and was elevated the following year to Domestic Prelate. He was consecrated Bishop on June 11, 1951, a year after he became National Director of the Society for the Propagation of the Faith. As a preacher he has been heard by millions in the United States, Canada and England, through the media of radio and television.

A prolific writer, he is author of two syndicated columns: "God Love You" for the Catholic press, and "Bishop Sheen Speaks," for the secular press; and is editor of two magazines: *Worldmission,* a quarterly review, and *Mission,* a bi-monthly. The popularity of his radio and television programs can be judged from the fact that his daily mail as a result of these programs has reached as much as ten thousand letters in a single day—about one-third of them from non-Catholics. The largest single delivery of mail after a program was thirty thousand letters. He conducted the first religious service ever telecast, served as narrator for a March of Time film, and has had his sermons issued in record album form. His interests are wide, and as well as serving on such organizations as the Catholic Literary Guild and the American Catholic Philosophical Society, he is an active member of the Mediaeval Academy and the American Geographical Association. The long list of his books started with publication of *God and Intelligence in Modern Philosophy* (Longmans, Green, 1925). This was followed by *Religion Without God* (Longmans, Green, 1928), *The Life of All Living* (Century, 1929), *The Divine Romance* (Century, 1930), *Old Errors and New Labels* (Century, 1931), *Moods and Truths* (Century, 1932), *The Way of the Cross* (Appleton-Century, 1933), *Seven Last Words* (Appleton-Century, 1933), *The Eternal Galilean* (Appleton-Century, 1934), *The Philosophy of Science* (Bruce, 1934), *The Mystical Body of Christ* (Sheed and Ward, 1935), *Calvary and the Mass* (Kenedy, 1936), *The Moral Universe* (Bruce, 1936), *The Cross and the Beatitudes* (Kenedy, 1937), *The Cross and the Crisis* (Bruce, 1938), *Liberty, Equality and Fraternity* (Macmillan, 1938), *The Rainbow of Sorrow* (Kenedy, 1938), *Victory Over Vice* (Kenedy, 1939), *Freedom Under God* (Bruce, 1949), *Whence Come Wars?* (Sheed and Ward, 1940), *The Seven Virtues* (Kenedy, 1940), *For God and Country* (Kenedy, 1941), *A Declaration of Dependence* (Bruce, 1941), *God and War* (Kenedy, 1942), *The Divine Verdict* (Kenedy, 1943), *The Armor of God* (Kenedy, 1943), *Philosophies at War* (Scribner's, 1943), *Seven Words to the Cross* (Kenedy, 1944), *Seven Pillars of Peace* (Scribner's, 1944), *Love One Another* (Kenedy, 1944), *Seven Words of Jesus and Mary* (Kenedy, 1945), *Preface to Religion* (Kenedy, 1946), *Characters of the Passion* (Kenedy, 1946), *Jesus, Son of Mary* (McMullen, 1947), *Communism and the Conscience of the West* (Bobbs, Merrill, 1948), *Philosophy of Religion* (Appleton-Century-Crofts, 1948), *Peace of Soul* (McGraw-Hill, 1949), *Lift Up Your Heart* (McGraw-Hill, 1950), *Three to Get Married* (Appleton-Century-Crofts, 1951), *The World's First Love* (McGraw-Hill, 1952), *Life Is Worth Living, First Series* (McGraw-Hill, 1953), *Life Is Worth Living, Second Series* (McGraw-Hill, 1954), *The Life of Christ* (McGraw-Hill, 1954), *The Way to Happiness* (Garden City, 1954), *Life Is Worth Living, Third Series* (McGraw-Hill, 1955), *The Way to Inner Peace* (Garden City, 1955), *God Love You* (Garden City, 1955), *Thinking Life Through* (Garden City, 1955), *The True Meaning of Christmas* (McGraw-Hill, 1955), *Life Is Worth Living, Fourth Series* (McGraw-Hill, 1956), *Thoughts for Daily Living* (Garden City, 1956), *Life Is Worth Living, Fifth Series* (McGraw-Hill, 1957), *This is the Mass* (Hawthorn, 1958), *This is Rome* (Hawthorn, 1960), *Go to Heaven* (McGraw-Hill, 1960), *This is the Holy Land* (Hawthorn, 1961), *These are the Sacraments* (Hawthorn, 1962), *The Fulton J. Sheen Sunday Missal* (Hawthorn, 1962), *The Priest is not His Own* (McGraw-Hill, 1963 and *The Power of Love* (McCall Magazine Corporation, 1964).

He is Auxiliary Bishop of New York and National Director of the Pontifical Society for the Propagation of the Faith.

Yousuf Karsh was born December 23, 1908, at Mardin, Armenia, and left for Canada at the age of fifteen during the Turkish Massacres. Son of an import-export entrepreneur and grandson of an engraver, he went to stay with an uncle, A. G. Nakash, who owned a photography studio in Sherbrooke, Quebec. He took an interest in the art of the camera and was sent by his uncle to Boston to study. After several years in the United States he went to open his own studio in Canada's capital, where within a few years he was photographing the cream of society and leaders of government. When war broke out in 1939, Ottawa became a center of Allied war activity and "Karsh of Ottawa" became a familiar signature on the portraits of some of the world's greatest leaders. His famous portrait of Winston Churchill in 1941 rocketed him to fame as the world's greatest portrait photographer, and that photograph, along with seventy-four others, taken in all parts of the world in the four years that followed, went into his first book, *Faces of Destiny* (Ziff-Davis, 1946). He followed this with *This is the Mass* (Hawthorn, 1958), *Portraits of Greatness* (Thomas Nelson & Sons, 1959), *This is Rome* (Hawthorn, 1960), *This is the Holy Land* (Hawthorn, 1961), *These are the Sacraments* (Hawthorn, 1962), and the publication of his memoirs, *In Search of Greatness* (Knopf, 1962). His latest work, *The Warren Court*, with John P. Frank, was published by the Macmillan Company in 1964. Still a world traveler, he keeps cameras and equipment at studios in London, Paris and New York, as well as in Ottawa, and usually carries a set of traveling equipment that weighs a minimum of 250 pounds. He always uses a white camera, finding that the traditional black is too depressing, and his focusing cloth varies in color with his own mood—though it is most often of red velvet with a gold satin lining. Groups of his portraits form part of the permanent collections of such museums as the Brooklyn Museum Department of Photography and the Museum of Modern Art in New York, Eastman House, Rochester, New York, the Art Institute of Chicago, and the Huntington Library, San Marino, California. In acknowledgment of his contribution to Canadian art and culture he received one of the first Canadian Citizenship Certificates in January, 1947, when Parliament passed a law creating Canadian citizenship. In May, 1960, both Queens University, Kingston, and Carleton University, Ottawa, conferred on Mr. Karsh honorary degrees of Doctor of Letters. Dartmouth College, Hanover, New Hampshire, honored him with the degree of Doctor of Humane Letters in June of 1961. Other awards include the bronze plaque of the Muscular Dystrophy Associations of America in September of 1964 and the Medal of the Royal Canadian Academy for notable contribution to Canadian arts in November of the same year.

In 1962 Mr. Karsh was married to Estrellita Nachbar in New York City.

Alastair Guinan was born in 1909. He received his early education privately in the United States, France, and England, largely under the direction of his Mother, who was a convinced disciple of the theories of François de Fénelon. Subsequently, he attended St. Benedict's College, Fort Augustus, Scotland, Mt. St. Mary's College in Maryland, and Columbia University in New York, where he was a pupil of the late Reverend Cornelius Cyprian Clifford, S.T.D. (Oenip.). From 1957 to 1962 he was Lecturer in English Language and Literature at Hunter College, New York; and in 1962–1963 he served as Master-in-Residence at the Cathedral School of St. Paul, Garden City, Long Island, New York. From 1959 to 1962, he was Lecturer in Communication Arts at Lenox Hill Hospital School of Nursing in New York. While at Hunter, he served as Vice-President of the Faculty Club and as a member of the Faculty-Student Committee of the Hunter College Conference on Religion in Life. Mr. Guinan has also lectured widely; and, since 1931, he has been a contributor to various British and American periodicals and learned journals. His writings include: "The Catholic Choir" (*American Ecclesiastical Review,* March, 1936); "The Worship of the Whole Man" (*The Month,* London, March 1937); "The Roman Ordo Sepeliendi Parvulos" (*Homiletic and Pastoral Review,* October 1939); "Our Lady's Intercessory Rôle in the Byzantine Liturgy" (*American Ecclesiastical Review,* November 1942); "Cornelius Cyprian Clifford, 1859–1938" (*The Catholic World,* October 1952); "Portrait of a Devout Humanist: M. l'Abbé Henri Brémond: An Essay Introductory to His Life and Thought" (*Harvard Theological Review,* January 1954); "Current Projects of Breviary Reform" (*Downside Review,* Bath, England, Winter 1954); "Our Lady as Intercessor for the Departed: A Glance at Liturgical Life under the Ancien Régime" (*Theological Studies,* September 1954); "The Christian Concept of Kingship as Manifested in the Liturgy of the Western Church: A Fragment in Suggestion" (*Harvard Theological Review,* October 1956); articles in

The Encyclopedia Americana: "Pius IX"; "Pius XII"; "Catholic Emancipation Act"; "Lateran Council"; "J. B. de La Salle," and other subjects in ecclesiastical history and biography; innumerable critical articles and reviews in *The Commonweal; The Polish Review; The Christian Science Monitor;* the London *Tablet; The Sword of the Spirit; Bonaventura* (Dublin); etc.; and he contributed the Introduction to Stepas Zobarskas: *The Maker of Gods: Ten Lithuanian Stories* (New York: Voyages Press, 1961). His principal translations (other than *This is the Mass*) are: André Combes: *Sainte Thérèse and Her Mission* (New York: Kenedy, 1955); R. L. Bruckberger: *Toward the Summit* (New York: Kenedy, 1956); Omer Englebert: *Catherine Labouré* (New York: Kenedy, 1959); *Pius XII (Eugenio Pacelli): The Complete Prayers of H.H. Pius XII, from the Original Texts* (New York: Desclée, 1959): Auguste Valensin: *Joy in the Faith: Meditations* (New York: Desclée, 1959); H. Daniel-Rops: *The Book of Mary* (New York: Hawthorn, 1960); H. Daniel-Rops: *The Second Vatican Council* (New York: Hawthorn, 1962). Mr. Guinan presently lives in New York, where he was married, in 1963, to Dr. Rose-Marie Daële, Chairman of the Department of Foreign Languages at Hunter College High School of the City University of New York, and Professor at the French University in New York. In addition to literature and liturgiology, Mr. Guinan's chief interests are in music, swimming, and horseback riding.